1/95

The Servant, the General and Armageddon

D1600682

The Servant, the General and Armageddon

by

Roderic Maude and Derwent Maude

George Ronald • Oxford

George Ronald, Publisher
46 High Street
Kidlington, Oxford OX5 2DN

© Roderic Maude and Derwent Maude 1998
All Rights Reserved

A Cataloguing-in-Publication entry is
available from the British Library

ISBN 0-85398-424-7

Cover illustration by Roderic Maude
Cover design by Barney Leith
Typesetting by Leith Editorial Services, Abingdon, Oxon, UK
Printed in Finland by WSOY

Contents

To Stephanie and Nora

Acknowledgements

We express our thanks to the Liddell Hart Centre for Military Archives, London, for permission to quote from the papers of Field-Marshal Viscount Allenby.

The stories and sayings in this book are, for the most part, the recollections of individuals – sometimes written down years after the events took place. It is therefore impossible to say for certain how accurate they are. This is true for the quoted sayings and talks of 'Abdu'l-Bahá as with the words of other individuals.

I

The Soldier's Vision

The third angel emptied his bowl into the rivers and water-springs and they turned into blood. Then I heard the angel of water say, 'You are the holy He-Is-and-He-Was, the Just One, and this is a just punishment: they spilt the blood of the saints and the prophets, and blood is what you have given them to drink; it is what they deserve.'

Revelation 16:4–6[1]

Palestine's long dry season was over. But the sun-baked earth, like a man parched from days without water, could accept only a few drops. The rain which splashed on the surface quickly flowed away down steep gullies and, when the sky cleared, only a mist remained clinging to the Judæan hills.

To soldiers on both sides of the conflict, thirst was a constant companion. It could drive men and horses mad – whether they be from Turkey or from England – and it would kill as surely as any bullet.

Two ancient wells were known to exist in a village just behind Turkish lines. The place had already changed hands four times in the preceding days. Many soldiers had died.[2] Now a new British attack was planned. If sudden and sustained, it might drive the defenders back, leaving the wells undamaged.

Every soldier knew the goal. But only the officers knew the grim calculation in which their lives had been weighed. It was a balance of blood for water.

The battle would be hard fought. The front line was almost in sight of the outskirts of Jerusalem. By that day in 1917 it had been almost seven hundred years since a Christian nation had come so close to controlling the site of Jesus' crucifixion. The whole region was resonant with significance. The attitude of the soldiers had gradually changed as the spiritual traditions of the country began to influence them.[3]

Religious fervour was not confined to one side. The city was holy to Muslims and Christians alike. The Turkish troops were well disciplined and, even though outnumbered, would defend bravely. For them it was a Holy War.

For one of the British officers, Wellesley Tudor Pole, the battle for the wells of Beit el Fokka was to have a special significance. In the thick of the fight he was to have a mystical experience that would change the course of his life.

In the few hours of peace that preceded the attack, Tudor Pole and his men looked out over the spectacular mountain scenery, keeping themselves well hidden behind their defences. It was a beautiful clear day.

At last the sun set and the stars shone in the velvet blackness. With the hillside engulfed in darkness, an order was given and the troops started to creep silently towards the Turkish front line at the top of the hill. It would be several hours before moonlight flooded the rocky slope. Groping in the dark and hampered by boulders, the men advanced a few yards at a time. Having come within half a mile of the summit, and with the crest of the hill still five hundred feet above them, the troops lay down and waited for the rising of the moon. The only sound was the distant cry of jackals.

It was only when the moon, almost full, appeared above the horizon that the country emerged out of blackness. Suddenly everything was clear, not just the rocky slope on which the troops lay, but the orange groves far away below them, the distant plains and beyond them the sea.

Tudor Pole surveyed the task ahead of them. First to clamber up the scrubby hillside, hampered by ravines and boulders. Then to cross the hill crest which had been roughly fortified. After that to run over a bare plateau devoid of sheltering cover. Finally to leap the stone walls of the old Roman village within which were the two precious wells.

He knew enough to take a shrewd guess at their chances of survival. 'I for one', he recalled, 'was satisfied that the enterprise was desperate.'[4]

The first wave of men began to creep slowly forward, just a few yards every five minutes. Tudor Pole was in the second wave, following close behind. Whilst picking his way silently, he heard shots in the distance, followed by silence. Then it started. Shrapnel shells burst in the air over his head, showering the ground with deadly fragments. Machine gun bullets strafed the rocks. The moonlight was in his eyes and he could not make out how many of the first wave had survived. Artillery shells started landing close by – so loud were they that the men could not hear the sound of their own voices. He saw soldiers dying around him. Some crumpled without even opening their mouths to cry out. Others groaned in agony before lying still.

The first wave had taken heavy casualties and the call came for reinforcements. Tudor Pole led his men forward.

Running in short bursts, they threw themselves over boulders, falling to the ground when they needed a few seconds to catch breath. There seemed to be Turkish snipers behind every rock, in every crevice and tree. Bullets whistled past them. Tudor Pole and his men fixed bayonets and leapt forward once more, killing many defenders as they ran.

On reaching the brow of the hill, they jumped the defences. It was then that the mystical experience started to take hold of Tudor Pole and he began to feel a sense of heightened consciousness.

'I was lifted', he recalled, ' . . . above the blood and hell around us.'[5]

Machine gun fire was raking the ledge on which the men lay. Suddenly a score of Turkish soldiers jumped, screaming, onto the ledge, to die at the hands of Tudor Pole's men.

'Don't shoot!' The cry came from the Turkish lines. Peering forward, Tudor Pole saw officers dressed in British khaki advancing towards his position. 'Don't shoot!' The words were called in good English. Perhaps Tudor Pole's men hesitated, but seeing hundreds of Turkish troops advancing behind the officers, they quickly understood that they were being tricked and continued to fire.

Having received orders not to advance further, they lay on the ledge and were picked off one by one. 'I felt a sudden premonition', Tudor Pole recalled, 'that a decision had been arrived at as to my own fate.'[6] He half stood to call for more men, then suddenly dropped back to his knees, blood pouring from a bullet wound. The sergeant hurried over to see what was wrong but he too caught a bullet and fell dead on top of Tudor Pole, pinning him to the ground.

Tudor Pole lay unconscious as the battle surged around him. During the night British troops somehow managed to capture the hill on which he lay. Then, as had happened twice before, Turkish machine gun fire raked them from the nearby hills until they were forced to pull back.[7]

The next thing Tudor Pole recalled was the silence as the sun rose over the Judæan mountains. It was bitterly cold and he longed for another bullet to put an end to the pain. The sergeant's body still lay heavily across him. He could raise his head but no more. There was no sign of life.

Then the firing began again. The Turkish soldiers were sweeping back over the hill bayonetting the wounded. To thwart the objective of the next British advance, they took many bodies and dumped them into the wells where the blood and water would mix and become one.

In a haze of pain, Tudor Pole felt an unseen presence kneeling next to him, telling him to place his head back on the ground. He obeyed. Then the Turkish soldiers arrived but passed quickly, leaving him for dead.

This strange experience of an unseen guardian led Tudor Pole to believe that there was a deep reason for his escape; that he was being entrusted with a mission, the nature of which he could not perceive. 'I was needed', he concluded, 'for some other work later on in life.'[8]

The strange experience continued as he lay still. Perhaps an hour passed before he felt he was being guided again, this time to move. He raised himself and found that the sergeant's body and rifle had rolled away and he was free. With the help of a stick, he drew himself into a crawling position.

Suffering from a serious bullet wound, he could not survive in the open for long. He needed medical attention.

He needed water. Time was running out.

Scuffling on hands and knees, he crawled across the dusty ground, following the prompting of his unseen guide, though with no clear sense of where he was going. Yard by agonizing yard he moved forward, coming at last to the shadowy entrance of a cave. Once more his life had been saved, for in the cave he found fresh water.

How he found his way back from the cave to the British lines we do not know, but once there he was rushed to hospital. The surgeon examined him and pronounced that the sniper's bullet had passed right through Tudor Pole's body without touching any vital organs or arteries and without breaking any bones. He concluded that it was not far short of a miracle.[9]

Tudor Pole's injuries put him out of the front line but not out of the war. After recovering, he was transferred to military intelligence where he interpreted reports coming from spies operating far behind the Turkish lines. Right from the start he received disturbing intelligence from the area just north of Mount Carmel. The commander of the Turkish 4th Army had vowed to crucify a certain religious leader in the event of a Turkish retreat from the district.[10]

The news might have seemed innocuous to any other British officer. The Turkish authorities had executed many prominent people in the region. All it needed was a suspicion that a person was working against the interests of the Ottoman Empire. But the man under threat was known to Tudor Pole and the news alarmed him deeply. The name of the religious leader was 'Abbás Effendi, better known around the world as 'Abdu'l-Bahá.

2

The Servant

When you hear of wars and rumours of wars, do not be alarmed, this is something that must happen, but the end will not be yet. For nation will fight against nation, and kingdom against kingdom. There will be earthquakes here and there; there will be famines. This is the beginning of the birthpangs.

Mark 13:7–8

'Abbás Effendi was the son of Bahá'u'lláh (an Arabic title meaning 'the Glory of God'), founder of the Bahá'í religion. The entire family had been banished from Persia when 'Abbás Effendi was just nine years old. From that time on, life was always hard and often dangerous. After three further banishments the family arrived in the prison city of Acre on Palestine's Mediterranean coast. Here they would remain.

With the passing of Bahá'u'lláh in 1892, 'Abbás Effendi became head of the Bahá'í religion. From that time on, He adopted the name 'Abdu'l-Bahá, which means 'Servant of the Glory'.[1]

'My name is 'Abdu'l-Bahá,' the Bahá'í leader explained, '. . . and servitude to all the human race my perpetual religion . . . No name, no title, no mention, no commendation have I, nor will ever have, except 'Abdu'l-Bahá.'[2]

It was only with the Young Turks' Revolution and a general amnesty that the imprisoned Bahá'ís were finally released. The year was 1908.[3]

'I was young when I was put into prison', recalled 'Abdu'l-Bahá, 'and my hair was white when the prison doors opened.'[4]

Major Tudor Pole well remembered his first meeting with the Bahá'í leader. It was in Egypt, four years before the outbreak of war. Though He was not tall, 'Abdu'l-Bahá's presence was striking. His hair and beard cascaded long and white over shoulder and chest. His eyes shone clear blue, a feature unusual among the people of Persia. Dressed in flowing eastern clothes and wearing a small white turban, 'Abdu'l-Bahá looked to many like an Old Testament prophet.

Knowing that the ageing religious leader had only just been released from confinement, Tudor Pole must have been concerned for 'Abdu'l-Bahá's welfare.

'Abdul-Baha's [sic] health had very greatly improved since his arrival from Port Said,' the Englishman observed. 'He was looking strong and vigorous in every way. He spoke much of the work in America, to which he undoubtedly is giving considerable thought.'[5]

Tudor Pole was to meet 'Abdu'l-Bahá again a year later. On 6 September 1911, *The Times* reported:

> BAHAI LEADER IN LONDON. Abdul Baha (Abbas Effendi), the leader of the Bahai movement, has arrived in London. He expects to remain about a fortnight in this country.[6]

The following Sunday 'Abdu'l-Bahá, still dressed in the eastern style, ascended the pulpit of a large London church and addressed the packed congregation. He gave the address in Persian and after it was finished Tudor Pole read out the English translation. The talk, which lasted only a few minutes, made a deep impression on the audience.

'O noble friends,' the Bahá'í leader began, 'seekers after God! Praise be to God! Today the light of Truth is shining upon the world in its abundance . . . The sea of the unity of mankind is lifting up its waves with joy, for there is real communication between the hearts and minds of men.'[7]

The message was optimistic and in sharp contrast to the political tensions gripping Europe. Everywhere were signs of military build-up. Armies were marching across Germany on manoeuvres. Italy was at war with Turkey in North Africa. The British navy was expanding.

Military hardware was developing rapidly and technological barriers were being overcome. That very week, the British navy was putting its new super-warship, *Orion*, through trials. The size of the guns was such that when they fired, concussion destroyed some of the non-essential fixtures on board. But, as the hull remained undamaged, the trials were hailed as a success.[8]

Nor did the threat of war concern only the military. Financial markets were having to cope with the uncertainty. The day after 'Abdu'l-Bahá's first talk, much insurance was being taken out against the risk of war between France and Germany. Lloyds of London started by pricing it at ten per cent of the sum being insured for cover until the end of the year. A few hours later the price had almost doubled.[9]

It was against this background that 'Abdu'l-Bahá's gave His address. The contrast could not be more striking.

'War shall cease between nations, and by the will of

God the Most Great Peace shall come; the world will be seen as a new world, and all men will live as brothers.'[10]

'Abdu'l-Bahá would continue for many months to travel and speak at public venues. It quickly became apparent that the Bahá'í leader was not blind to the complexities of the situation. He clearly anticipated an approaching conflict – but also saw beyond it to a time of universal peace.

'By what process', one questioner asked, 'will this peace on earth be established? Will it come at once after a universal declaration of the Truth?'

'No,' 'Abdu'l-Bahá replied, 'it will come about gradually. A plant that grows too quickly lasts but a short time. You are my family,' He looked about, with a smile, 'my new children! If a family lives in unison, great results are obtained. Widen the circle; when a city lives in intimate accord greater results will follow, and a continent that is fully united will likewise unite all other continents. Then will be the time of the greatest results, for all the inhabitants of the earth belong to one native land.'[11]

'Abdu'l-Bahá met many of the prominent people of the day, such as the Lord Mayor of London and Archdeacon Wilberforce. He also took the time and effort to visit some of the poorest people. Throughout His stay there was a stream of visitors: clergy from several different religions, diplomats, reporters, academics, royalty, members of the aristocracy, politicians, leading suffragettes, Esperantists, Theosophists and others.

International tensions heightened as the weeks passed. The danger was fuelled by both old national rivalries and the rapid development of new military technology. The Italian army had just started using aeroplanes for reconnaissance. It would not take long for the other military uses of flight to be discovered. Political cartoons were already referring to the alarming military build-up in terms of 'Armageddon'.

On 20 October 1911 the Italian army captured a town in North Africa. 'Abdu'l-Bahá, by then in France, learned of the fighting.

'The news of the Battle of Benghazi grieves my heart . . .' the Bahá'í leader announced to an audience the following day. 'I charge you all that each one of you concentrate all the thoughts of your heart on love and unity. When a thought of war comes, oppose it by a stronger thought of peace . . .

'In this room today are members of many races, French, American, English, German, Italian, brothers and sisters meeting in friendship and harmony! Let this gathering be a foreshadowing of what will, in very truth, take place in this world . . .'[12]

On 1 November Italian aeroplanes took off from their base in North Africa, flew across the front line and dropped bombs on Turkish troops defending the Tanguira Oasis.

In December, with the cold weather closing in, 'Abdu'l-Bahá returned to Egypt. The exertion of the previous four months had left its mark. A period of relative rest was needed.

'Abdu'l-Bahá set out again in the spring of 1912, this time for America.[13] The journey across America would last eight months, extend over five thousand miles and encompass at least 139 public talks. 'Abdu'l-Bahá, 68 years old and in failing health, also took on a heavy itinerary of personal interviews with people from all walks of life and maintained a constant stream of correspondence.

The sight of the ageing Persian with a small entourage of secretaries, translators and assistants, made a deep impression on those who saw it. Many people considered 'Abdu'l-Bahá to be a prophet or even the return of Christ. He denied this emphatically.

Under a headline of 'PROPHET'S DASH FOR TRAIN' the *New York Times* ran the following story:

> Montclair, N.J. June 29 – The departure of Abdul Baha, leader of the Bahaist cult, from Montclair to-day was attended by excitement. Abdul Baha and a retinue of ten fez-wearing Persians had been staying at 11 Bradford Place for several weeks. Arrangements were made for the departure of the aged prophet to-day for West Englewood . . . Several members of his retinue left for the Lackawanna station in advance of their leader.
>
> When train time came, Abdul Baha was not in sight. He had been delayed. The baggage of the Persians was aboard the train, and as it moved away they appealed to the trainmen in several Oriental languages to defer the departure for a few minutes. Several of the excited followers of the prophet, when they realized that the train was leaving, jumped to the platforms. One of them, in swinging his arms about, accidentally or otherwise, pulled the bell rope. At the same instant, by a strange coincidence, Abdul Baha hove in sight in an automobile. To add to the excitement a Persian accidentally knocked off the conductor's hat. The train came to a halt, and Abdul Baha leaped from the automobile and was hustled aboard the coach by his friends.[14]

In all 'Abdu'l-Bahá did and said on the speaking tour, the urgent and pressing need for peace was constantly repeated. The newspapers quickly caught the message. The New York press was first to take up the story: 'PERSIAN

TEACHER OF WORLD-PEACE IS HERE', 'ABDUL BAHA HERE TO
CONVERT AMERICA TO HIS PEACE DOCTRINE'.[15]

During His tour the Bahá'í leader spoke to both peace
societies and military men.

'I understand you are a messenger of peace to this
country,' said Hudson Maxim, inventor of smokeless
explosives, delayed action fuses and torpedo propellants.

'You are a celebrated inventor and scientific expert',
'Abdu'l-Bahá told him, 'whose energies and faculties are
employed in the production of means for human destruction . . . Now you have the opportunity of becoming
doubly famous. You must practise the science of peace . . .
invent guns of love which shall shake the foundations of
humanity.'[16]

But 'Abdu'l-Bahá's call for peace was not simplistic.
Sometimes speaking at five meetings in a single day, the
Bahá'í leader repeatedly and systematically outlined principles which He claimed would tackle the root causes of
war.

Among these was the equality of the sexes. With the
issue of women's suffrage high on the political agenda, this
was bound to be picked up by the media. 'BANISHED FIFTY
YEARS, LEADER OF BAHAI HERE: PERSIAN PHILOSOPHER FAVORS
WOMEN SUFFRAGE AND WILL TALK PEACE'.[17]

Speaking in Pittsburgh, 'Abdu'l-Bahá made the connection explicit.

In past ages humanity has been defective and inefficient
because it has been incomplete. War and its ravages have
blighted the world; the education of woman will be a
mighty step toward its abolition and ending, for she will
use her whole influence against war . . . In truth, she will
be the greatest factor in establishing universal peace and

international arbitration. Assuredly, woman will abolish warfare among mankind.[18]

Owing to His view on sexual equality, 'Abdu'l-Bahá met many of the leading suffragettes, both in Britain and America. In one of these encounters, Mrs Emily Pankhurst suggested that the Bahá'í leader was a Prophet. 'Oh, no!' 'Abdu'l-Bahá exclaimed, smiling broadly. 'I am a man, like you.'[19]

On 12 May 1912 'Abdu'l-Bahá spoke to the International Peace Forum saying: 'Just now Europe is a battlefield of ammunition ready for a spark, and one spark will set aflame the whole world.'[20]

On 29 May Greece and Bulgaria signed an Anti-Ottoman Alliance. The network of alliances and pacts linking European nations was becoming ever more tangled. The situation was made even more dangerous because many of these agreements were secret. Serbia joined the Anti-Ottoman Alliance in June. On 22 July Britain recalled some of its warships from the Mediterranean to counter a build-up of the German navy.

On 16 September 1912 'Abdu'l-Bahá gave a specific warning:

Conditions are becoming acute, drawing nigh unto the degree of men warring upon the seas, warring upon the plains, warring in the very atmosphere with a violence unknown in former centuries.[21]

With tension growing in the Balkans, on 8 October Montenegro declared war on the Ottoman Empire. Six days later the Turks invaded Serbia and five days after that the allied Balkan armies invaded Turkey.

City by city, 'Abdu'l-Bahá travelled through the United

States and Canada, reaching California in October. The
wave of media interest still surged around the Bahá'í
leader. 'ABDUL BAHA BRINGS GOSPEL OF PEACE', 'NOTED
PERSIAN IS HERE TO PLEAD FOR PEACE'.[22]

On 26 October 'Abdu'l-Bahá's dark warnings were
repeated with more detail.

> The European continent is like an arsenal, a storehouse of
> explosives ready for ignition . . . particularly at this time
> when the Balkan question is before the world.[23]

As the political situation in Europe deteriorated it became
ever clearer that a huge pan-continental war was close.
That very month 'Abdu'l-Bahá made a chilling prediction.
'We are on the eve of the Battle of Armageddon referred
to in the sixteenth chapter of Revelation.' What images of
terror that must have conveyed to the audience! But this
was more than a vague allusion. He continued: 'The time
is two years hence, when only a spark will set aflame the
whole of Europe . . . By 1917 kingdoms will fall and cata-
clysms will rock the earth.'[24]

While still in America, 'Abdu'l-Bahá cabled Palestine,
giving specific instructions for the Bahá'ís to start preparing to weather the coming storm.

On 5 December 1912 'Abdu'l-Bahá set sail on His
return journey. Visiting first England, France, Germany
and Austria, the Bahá'í leader returned at last to Egypt. He
stayed for five and a half months near Alexandria, receiving a stream of guests from the East and West. On 29 June
1913 'Abdu'l-Bahá instructed the last visitors to leave.[25]
'Abdu'l-Bahá arrived back in Haifa on 5 December 1913.[26]

On 28 June 1914, with the Balkan crisis at boiling point,
a Serbian nationalist shot and killed Archduke Franz Ferdi-

nand in Sarajevo. Claiming the Serbs had complicity in the murder, Austria-Hungary declared war on them in retaliation. A half hidden network of secret treaties and old alliances then pulled in the other European nations one after the other and the world was at war.

3

The General

The seventh angel emptied his bowl into the air, and a voice shouted from the sanctuary, 'The end has come'. Then there were flashes of lightning and peals of thunder and the most violent earthquake that anyone has ever seen since there have been men on the earth.

Revelation 16:17–18

From the time of Napoleon, no armed conflict on European soil had lasted for more than a few weeks. Blind to the reality of modern warfare, many people still looked forward to a short and glorious conflict with eager anticipation.[1] Crowds cheered when, in the summer of 1914, war was declared and volunteers came forward to enlist in the British army.

But hopes of glory were soon past. Dreams of honour were trampled into the quagmire of the trenches. Millions were killed or mutilated. Some were shot, some gassed, others drowned in mud-filled craters.

'Abdu'l-Bahá was filled with agony at the news of human slaughter. Palestine was not cut off from the outside world. From the precincts of Bahá'u'lláh's shrine, just outside Acre, the Bahá'í leader wrote a series of long letters to the Bahá'ís of America and Canada, calling on them to continue to promote the cause of peace.

> Now this is the time that you may arise and perform this
> most great service and become the cause of the guidance
> of innumerable souls. Thus through this superhuman
> service the rays of peace and conciliation may illumine
> and enlighten all the regions and the world of humanity
> may find peace and composure.[2]

He continued to identify the events of the war with the
battle of Armageddon.

> During my stay in America I cried out in every meeting
> and summoned the people to the propagation of the
> ideals of universal peace. I said plainly that the continent
> of Europe had become like unto an arsenal and its confla-
> gration was dependent upon one spark, and that in the
> coming years, or within two years, all that which is
> recorded in the Revelation of John and the Book of
> Daniel would become fulfilled and come to pass.[3]

The first five of these letters were published in America in
early September 1916. After that, communication between
the Holy Land and the outside world was severed. The following spring America entered the war.

The officer who was to send his forces to fight for the wells
of Beit el Fokka, the battle in which Tudor Pole would be
wounded, was General Edmund H.H. Allenby. Though it
was only late in his military career that Allenby learned of
'Abdu'l-Bahá, fate was to bring the two men together.

Allenby was a tall, broad-shouldered, square-jawed
man possessed of great physical strength. He wore his
receding hair cut very short and sported a thick, neatly

trimmed moustache. His manner was brusque, almost to the point of rudeness. Both in build and personality, he was a man difficult to ignore.

The general's first experience of fighting had been during the Boer War in South Africa. It was there that his skills and intelligence had first shone. He had the knack of coming through dangerous situations with few casualties. It was an ability which won the affection of the men who served under him and the admiration of the higher officers.

In South Africa, Allenby quickly acquired a reputation which had him in constant demand. There was little time to rest and repair equipment. Writing to his wife, Allenby lamented the situation. 'My coat just keeps going', he observed, 'but it was badly eaten by white ants a fortnight ago, and is now very well ventilated. My servant has patched it here and there with what looks like parts of a brown sock.'[4]

> We got in here after a very hard week . . . We are in a beastly bivouac, tentless, blanketless, unwashed and dusty . . . My property now consists of the dirty clothes I live and sleep in day and night, a cloak, a saddle blanket, a toothbrush, a box of cigarettes and a tube of lanoline. On the march I lived chiefly on biscuit and beef tongues. The horses are half starved. Rhodes is behaving very well. He sent our men soup, firewood, etc. I dined with him last night.[5]

According to the mood of the time, soldiers were expected to welcome war, to look forward to a fierce and glorious fight. Even at the start of his South African adventure, Allenby felt he was falling short of this ideal. 'I am coming to the conclusion', he confided, 'that I have too happy a life at home to make a really good soldier. I catch myself often half-hoping that the war may be won by the time we arrive . . .'[6]

By 1900 he felt more strongly about it and was stating bluntly, 'I hate war'.[7] And later, 'I feel more deadly sick of the war every day. My martial ardour, which was always a somewhat feeble flicker, has quite burnt out.'[8]

Allenby learned much during the Boer War; the importance of water, the need for good intelligence, the value of seeing things with his own eyes and of respecting those against whom he fought. He also learned that things were not as they ought to have been in the British army.

He returned to England with the determination to rise to a point where he had the authority to institute changes. It was an uphill struggle and it took a toll on him.

'It cannot be denied', noted one admirer, 'that in Allenby increasing authority brought increasing asperity. He who had been a noticeably easy-going young officer and a good-humoured squadron commander was a strict colonel, an irascible brigadier, and an explosive general.'[9]

By the autumn of 1916 Allenby was deeply involved with the war on the western front. He was a professional soldier and would follow orders from above – however foolish they seemed. This did not make him very popular with those below him who suffered the results, but Sir John French, the Commander in Chief, thought sufficiently well of him to appoint Allenby to the rank of full general. Shortly afterwards, Sir John French was replaced by General Douglas Haig.

Haig had definite views on the war. He believed that things were going well. It was true that vast numbers of his men were losing their lives, but the Germans, he was sure, were suffering worse. He was resigned to a war of attrition.

Allenby disagreed. He was a cavalry officer at heart and longed for the single decisive breakthrough. The two men did not get on well.

At last, in 1917, Haig gave Allenby a chance to show what he could do in planning and commanding an operation. Allenby was to push forward the British troops from the town of Arras. It was to be a diversionary attack, drawing attention away from a larger French offensive.

Many of the contending generals throughout history seem to have believed that God was on their side. In contemplating the forthcoming offensive, General Haig was no exception. 'As to the Battle of Arras,' he observed, 'I know quite well that I am being used as a tool in the hands of a Divine Power.'[10]

The town of Arras lay just behind the front line, in territory controlled by the British army. By that time most of the buildings had been reduced to rubble. Things were different under the surface. A network of tunnels had been dug to connect cellars and natural caves to form a complex big enough to accommodate 25,000 men. It was lit with electric lights (a novel contrivance for the time) and had piped water. There was even an underground tram system.

Tunnels dug eastward from the underground city emerged between the front lines in no man's land. The Germans would only be aware of the advancing British soldiers at the last moment.

Tanks, tear gas and poison gas would be used for the attack. Smoke shells, only just developed to the point where they could be fired on a large scale, were also to be employed.

The plans Allenby submitted to General Headquarters had some distinctive and unusual features.

Firstly, the men were to be well fed and rested. In Allenby's own words, they were to be given 'a satisfactory breakfast before attacking – care is to be taken that this meal is a good one'.[11]

Secondly, the plan gave top priority to transport and good traffic control. (In practice, transport proved to be one of the biggest problems of the attack, not least because of the inadequate supply of rocks for road building and repair. It was difficult for the transport officers to understand how stones could be more important than ammunition.)

Finally, and most controversial of all, to ensure surprise there would only be a limited bombardment before the attack. On this point there was a strong disagreement with Haig. The minimum artillery barrage in such circumstances was usually a week. Allenby wanted an extremely intense bombardment lasting only 48 hours. Allenby hoped that the plan might catch the German defence unprepared because nothing of the kind had been tried before.

GHQ objected to the plan for exactly the same reason – nothing of the kind had been tried before. They said that, with the sustained rate of fire which the plan required, the gun crews would become exhausted and the guns themselves would overheat. Allenby retorted that his artillery chief, General Holland, had already experimented and found that a rapid rate of fire could be maintained if the gun crews were alternated and rest periods rigidly adhered to. The guns themselves would stand the use so long as the rate of fire was similarly strictly controlled.

Haig's GHQ responded by transferring General Holland to another sector. Holland was replaced by Robert Lecky, a man whom many regarded as 'the worst type of Horse Artillery commander' and 'the laughing stock of the regiment'.[12] In the eyes of GHQ, Lecky had one distinct advantage over Holland – he did not believe that Allenby's plan was possible.

Allenby was cornered. He had no choice but to agree to a longer bombardment but still managed to negotiate it down to a period of four days. He installed a large number of artillery pieces to compensate for the lower firing rate – one for every twelve yards of front line.

Haig was unhappy about all these unorthodox tactics which Allenby proposed. On the eve of the attack he sent a message saying that he had no faith in the plan and that if it were a failure Allenby would have to go.[13]

At 6.30 a.m. on the 4th of April 1917, the British artillery started firing, carpeting the German territory. The effect was psychologically devastating: the constant threat of sudden death, the nerve shattering flash and roar of explosions, the shaking of the earth, hour after hour, day after day. Shell shock, though presumed by many senior officers to be an excuse for malingering, was a very real condition, leaving men unable to perform the simplest task such as tying their shoe laces.

'We are existing in the grave!' exclaimed one of the German defenders. 'Horror on horror! Driven from splendid positions, what can our end be in this valley harried by the iron hail that crashes down incessantly? Even the approach trenches have fallen in, everything is churned up, with entire platoons lost in the debris in the front lines. When a relief comes it can not dig because of the bodies. We dare no longer go forward – and we crouch in the shellholes suffering prodigious losses pulverized by the terrible and continuous English drum fire.'[14]

After the bombardment started, the French general delayed the attack and Allenby was forced to maintain his bombardment for yet another day. Two million seven hundred thousand shells were fired during the bombardment. Though many of the German defences were destroyed, any chance of surprise had gone.

Just after dawn on Easter Monday, 9 April, the men emerged from their tunnels and started to advance. Squalls of snow started to fall from a dark sky. Feet and vehicles quickly churned the sodden earth into a quagmire and Allenby's transport system almost ground to a halt.

'The congestion on the road to Arras was bad enough,' recalled one eyewitness, 'but beyond that it is almost indescribable.'[15]

At first the attack was very successful, giving the largest advance for a single day that had been experienced in the war. On the second day the advance slowed. On the third it stopped.

Haig then intervened, giving fresh orders – which were misunderstood. By the fifth day, after very heavy losses, Haig called a halt to the advance. Pressure was maintained on the German lines until 5 May when, with more than 130,000 British soldiers killed, wounded or missing, the Battle of Arras was brought to a close.

Three of Allenby's generals had made formal protests about him during the battle.[16] Soon after, Allenby was summoned to London.

4

Sinai

The fourth angel emptied his bowl over the sun and it was made to scorch people with its flames; but though people were scorched by the fierce heat of it, they cursed the name of God who had power to cause such plagues, and they would not repent and praise Him.

Revelation 16:8–9

The Ottoman Empire had grown outward from Turkey over a period of almost seven hundred years. By the beginning of the 20th century it included all the territory of modern-day Israel, Jordan, Lebanon, Syria and Iraq – an empire even greater than the Babylonian Empire which had long ago flourished in the same area.

The people of Turkey were proud of their ancient empire. Many were patriots, willing to sacrifice for the good of the nation. Before 1914 Turkey had wanted to build a modern navy. Instead of the money being raised by taxes, it was given freely through voluntary contributions of the Turkish people. Much of it was collected door to door. Women cut off and sold their hair, lotteries were run and fairs organized. At last enough money was raised and the payments made, including money for two ironclad battleships from Britain.

No action could have been calculated as a greater snub,

therefore, when the British government, feeling nervous about Turkey's neutrality, confiscated the ships before they sailed. 'Never, never shall I forget my mental anguish when I heard this frightful news,' said Djemal Pasha, Turkey's Marine Minister.[1]

Germany promptly offered to loan the Turkish navy two of her own ships. The incident was enough to push Turkey into the war on the side of the Central Powers, fighting against Britain and her allies.

In February 1915 soldiers from the Turkish 4th Army, under the command of Djemal Pasha, set out west from Beersheba with the audacious aim of crossing the Sinai desert and capturing the Suez Canal from Britain. To raise morale and public support for the endeavour, the Turkish leaders persuaded Muslim clerics to designate the endeavour as a holy war, or *jihad*.

It was an extraordinary plan: upwards of 25,000 men and 14,000 camels, carrying and dragging pontoon bridges, gun batteries, field hospitals, telegraph equipment, food supplies and, above all, water.[2]

By day the sun was so bright that men could not tell one colour from another; by night the moonlight transformed the land into a patchwork of black and silver.

Marching only at night, packing planks and brushwood under the wheels of the heavy guns so they would not sink into the sand, they crossed more than one hundred miles of the least hospitable land on the planet. Food and water were rationed severely. The men survived mostly on biscuits, together with some dried fruit and olives.

The army arrived at the Suez Canal in early February 1915. The British knew of the advance but had underestimated it. Even though heavily outnumbered, the Turks managed to launch three pontoon bridges and send a force of some 600 men across to the far bank.

Though Djemal Pasha afterwards claimed that the attack was no more than a demonstration, he clearly hoped that Egyptian Arabs would rise in support of Turkey and that Britain would be defeated.

The Arab uprising did not come. The troops who had crossed the canal were all killed or captured. Although Djemal's adventure had failed, he congratulated the troops on their successful 'offensive reconnaissance against the canal'. He then led the main body of men back across the desert into Palestine. They were not pursued. Djemal had proved that an army could cross the Sinai.

The British would now be forced to keep a large force on standby in Egypt to defend the Suez Canal from a second attack. Men and resources were poured into the task. Trenches, bunkers and barricades were built. When Lord Kitchener came to inspect the defences in 1915, he saw the army pinned down, waiting for a smaller force to attack it. The irony was not lost on him. 'Are you defending the canal', he asked, 'or is the canal defending you?'

A second Turkish attack came in the summer of 1916. 'Brave soldiers,' said Djemal, 'you are going into the desert. I ask you to have patience and perseverance. You will return bearing your arms in victory, or you will leave your bones in the desert. Everything is bad in the desert, hunger, nakedness, dirt, every privation, therefore, I ask you to have courage and perseverance, O my soldiers.'[3]

Having heard the words of their commander, soldiers from the Turkish army, together with German troops, set out once more across the desert.

The commanders of the British and allied forces in

Egypt knew that the Turkish army was pushing south again. But even with spotter planes, finding out exactly where it was proved difficult. Troops on the ground seemed almost invisible from the air, so long as they spread out when they heard the aeroplane approaching and remained motionless as it flew overhead.

One Australian cavalryman recorded a typical event in his diary:

> May 20th . . . Last night a fool airman brought in information that two thousand Germans and seventeen hundred Turks were advancing on the post. We stood to arms from two o'clock this morning. I would have been off duty, so bang went my dreams of a few hours sleep; I cursed everything – everything!

No attack came that night.

> These aeroplane reports are 'fishy'. A fortnight ago, one reported that fifteen hundred Turks were advancing on Railhead. It turned out to be a gang of Egyptian labourers . . . The trouble is, we have to ride out and lose sleep over the myths.[4]

It was a game of desert hide-and-seek played by outriders from both sides. 'On patrol this morning . . .' recorded the Australian cavalryman.

> The sun rose a ball of quivering fire, hurrying from the east a wind straight from a furnace. The horses bent their heads and gasped . . . Some of B Squadron have collapsed after yesterday's patrol. They had a terrible trip.

> July 24th – Yesterday, very early, we rode out to Sumara Oasis. We were queerly shocked to find there were no

Turks there. We heard them though, to the east. Boom-oom-oomm! Boom-oom-oomm! then the rattle of musketry and the rut tut tut-tuttuttutut as the machine guns formed the chorus.[5]

The intensity of fighting escalated as the days passed:

August 1st . . . Nightly, the Turks advance a few miles across the desert – thousands of men in far-flung waves – the first wave sheer desert fighters and noiseless – they seem to arise out of the sand in overwhelming numbers . . . Under the brilliant starlight, the Turks when arising from among the bushes appear like transparent shadow men . . .[6]

Even though the Turks and Germans fought hard, they were not able to reach the canal a second time. And when they started to retreat across Sinai, the British and allied forces pressed forward in counter attack. The retreat became a chaotic withdrawal with supplies and equipment abandoned.

Now the British generals pushed eastward towards Palestine. Sand, flies, heat and thirst were never far away. The men were retracing a journey recorded in the Old Testament several thousand years before. 'Why did you bring us out of Egypt?' the Israelites had asked. 'Was it so that I should die of thirst, my children too, and my cattle?'[7]

But at last Sinai was crossed. 'I wish words were eyes and ears and feelings . . .' wrote the Australian cavalryman on reaching the edge of Palestine. 'Presently came shouts from the head of the column – men were standing in their stirrups pointing across the desert. Our horses pressed on. Then we saw them. Scarlet poppies! Wild flowers and scarlet poppies . . . Could this really be the end of the ever-lasting desert!'[8]

But the advance had taken time and the Turks, with German assistance, had started to prepare a line of fortifications running from Gaza on the Mediterranean coast to Beersheba in the Judæan hills. Trenches, sand bags, machine guns: all that had been learned through the bloody fighting in France was put into the Turkish defences.

'The great advantage of this position', Djemal Pasha observed, 'was that it could not be turned, as the right flank rested on the sea and the left on the desert.'[9]

On 27 March 1917 British and allied forces attacked Gaza. While cavalry attempted to encircle the town to cut off possible reinforcements, the infantry advanced towards the trenches. The men were utterly exposed to crossfire from machine guns and rifles. They sprang up from cover and ran forward towards the guns then threw themselves down to the ground to shoot. Another wave of attackers would then emerge from cover and run forward, not stopping until they were ahead of the last wave. Slowly, and taking terrible casualties, the infantry advanced. Then, at close range, they fought hand to hand with bayonets fixed.

Hour after hour the fighting continued until, at sunset, it looked as if the Turks had been defeated. But the British generals far behind the front line could not see what the troops knew – that they had all but succeeded in taking Gaza. They sent out the order to retreat.

When the call to pull back was sounded, the front line soldiers were astounded. Some asked for the message to be repeated, for they could not believe the stupidity of the order. The signal came again and again. 'Retire! Retire! Retire!'[10]

5

The Promised Land

Let the wilderness and the dry lands exult,
let the wasteland rejoice and bloom,
let it bring forth flowers like jonquil,
let it rejoice and sing for joy.

The glory of Lebanon is bestowed upon it,
the splendour of Carmel and Sharon;
they shall see the glory of Yahweh,
the splendour of our God.

Isaiah 35:1–2

General Smuts, fresh from a reasonably successful campaign in South Africa, had no intention of being sidelined any longer. The command of the Eastern Expeditionary Force was not an appealing prospect.

The army he was being asked to lead was stuck on the southern border of Palestine and taking heavy casualties. After the first disastrous battle for Gaza, a second attack had been launched. But the Turkish troops had repaired their defences and been reinforced by thousands of fresh men. Once more the British were pushed back.

As far as General Smuts was concerned, the war would be won or lost in Europe – that was the belief of the 'Westerners', which included most of the British top brass. The Palestine adventure was viewed as a sideshow which diverted men and resources from the real conflict.

The general recalled a conversation with the Chief of the Imperial General Staff: 'Sir William said to me, quite frankly, that if I were to accept the offer under the impression that something first-class could be done in Palestine, I would be making a great mistake, and he would dissuade me from accepting the command under such an impression.'[1]

Lloyd George, the British Prime Minister, was an 'Easterner'. He believed that the defeat of Turkey would have a dramatic effect on the morale of both sides. He also believed that by tackling Turkey, one of the props that supported Germany would be knocked away. He wanted a capable general to lead the Eastern Expeditionary Force. The trouble was, none of the really good officers would accept the offer.

At last General Smuts agreed – on the condition that he be allowed to land a large army on the coast behind Turkish lines. Such a plan had already been rejected in 1914 – and again in 1915, a fact that was almost certainly known to Smuts. The condition could not be accepted.

Smuts was off the hook. Another general was needed.

Lloyd George wanted a forceful character to lead the Eastern Expeditionary Force. There was no one more forceful in the British army than 'the Bull', as Allenby was known. Giving Allenby the job would achieve two things at a single stroke. Not only was he dynamic enough to breathe new life into the moribund eastern campaign, but separating him from General Haig would remove a source of friction from the western front.

Allenby was a 'Westerner', like most of the officers, and

the transfer seemed to him like a slap in the face. When an officer of high rank was removed, they did not say he was being demoted or punished – the suggestion would have been bad for the morale of the men. Instead, an incompetent officer would be 'unstuck'. Allenby was being unstuck – at least that was what he assumed.

It was not until he talked to Lloyd George that he started to change his mind. Haig and Lloyd George had very different ideas on how a war should be fought.

'I am trying to work in harmony with Lloyd George,' said Haig, 'but he has such strange ideas on warfare.'[2]

Lloyd George objected to the death of thousands of men for the gain of only a few miles of blasted mud – but then, he was a politician and not a military man.

The prime minister charmed Allenby and helped him take on board some of the Easterner's philosophy. Allenby was to have far more freedom than he was used to. The policy of that entire theatre would not be decided by the War Cabinet until he had assumed control and made an appreciation. Allenby was told to ask for all the reinforcements and supplies he needed.

'If you do not ask it will be your fault,' said Lloyd George. 'If you do ask and do not get what you need, it will be ours.'

The prime minister added that he expected 'Jerusalem before Christmas'.[3]

He then presented Allenby with a book, *The Historical Geography of the Holy Land*. It was a gift which must have been deeply appreciated for it was Allenby's habit to prepare for any task by reading. He sought out and studied all the literature he could find on Palestine, including the Old and New Testaments. Perhaps it was here that he began to understand the historical and contemporary significance of the region.

The place where the continents of Africa, Asia and Europe join had been a strategic trade route for the entire span of human history. It had also been a battle ground. It had been conquered by a succession of empires, but no empire had been based there. Four of the great world religions, encompassing nearly 40 per cent of the world's population, considered it holy.

Any overland trade between the entire Eurasian landmass and the great continent of Africa was squeezed into a narrow coastal strip between the Mediterranean Sea to the west and the burning desert of the Arabian peninsula to the east – a north-south corridor no more than a hundred miles wide. Through this narrow strip the tides of history surged, bringing armies and dispersing religious teachings.

This vital corridor has a simple topography composed of narrow north-south strips running parallel to the coast. On a journey inland from the sea a traveller would cross these strips in succession. First a ribbon of dunes and marshes, next a fertile plane, then a climb up into the Judæan hills, on one of which stands the city of Jerusalem. After this the land falls away sharply into a very deep valley in which are the Dead Sea, the River Jordan and the Sea of Galilee. The journey would finally grind to a halt in the mountains and deserts of the Arabian peninsula.

This simple pattern of parallel ridges and valleys is cut by Mount Carmel. The line of the mountain runs southeast from Haifa on the coast to join the Judæan hills just north of Jerusalem. It is a natural defensive barrier across the coastal plain.

The principal route by which this barrier may be crossed is the Musmus Pass, at the north end of which lies the town of Megiddo. Thus over the span of human history much of the trade between three continents was constrained to move through this area. The Old Testament tells of many battles on the plane of Esdraelon just to the north of Megiddo. The Bible also refers to the mountains around Megiddo – the Hebrew form of the Greek 'Armageddon'.

Allenby, a religious man, knew of the prophecies in the book of Revelation. The Battle of Armageddon was usually understood as the supreme conflict before the Kingdom of Heaven was to be established: a warning and a promise. To some people it was symbolic, to others a literal description of events yet to come.

In the early years of the 19th century, many Christian groups had used prophecy to predict that Christ was due to return. The German 'Temple Society' was one such group. The Templers (not to be confused with the Crusader Knights of the Temple) had been so convinced that the events described in the Bible were soon to happen that whole communities of them sold up their homes and moved to Palestine to wait. There they established small colonies living as they thought true Christians should.

Christians were not the only ones expecting the momentous events foretold in scripture. Muslims too were in a state of millennial excitement, waiting for the arrival of the 'Promised One'. Believing the event to be close at hand, some Islamic scholars urged people to prepare themselves and at least one sent his followers out across the Middle East in search.[4]

The Jews had been excluded from Palestine since 135 AD. Though scattered throughout the world, they never forgot the goal of returning to the land which they believed had been given to them by God. They had to wait until the 19th century for this dream to start to come true. They finally began to return in significant numbers in the 1840s. With the stream of returning Jews growing ever larger, fears were raised that they might be trying to establish a new state of Israel, an event synonymous in the Jewish scriptures with the long-expected coming of the Messiah.

The European powers had been in the Holy Land before. Waves of Christian armies had swept south to do battle with the Muslims for control of Jerusalem. These were wars fought in the heat of religious fervour. When in 1099 the Christians finally took the Holy City, they slaughtered all its inhabitants, including the women and children.

One of the Crusaders' most important military bases was the fortified city of St Jean d'Acre, on the coast nine miles north of Haifa. It subsequently came under the control of the Turkish Ottoman Empire. In the 18th century it was a centre of military power. In the early part of the 19th century the harbour silted up and its significance was reduced. By the middle of the 19th century, the harsh climate had combined with pollution, bad water, disease and decay to make the city of Acre a place foul beyond description. A local proverb stated that if a bird were to fly over the city it would drop dead from the stench. No longer were Acre's massive stone walls used for keeping invaders out. The city had become a Turkish penal colony. Within its walls some of the worst criminals of the Ottoman Empire were confined.

In 1868 a group of prisoners arrived from far off Persia. Chief among them was the founder of the Bahá'í religion, Bahá'u'lláh. The rest, 67 in all, were followers and family. 'Abdu'l-Bahá, then just 24 years old, was among them.

6

Famine and Plague

A ration of corn for a day's wages, and three rations of barley for a day's wages, but do not tamper with the oil or the wine.

Revelation 6:6

Almost eight hundred years after the Crusaders took Jerusalem, history seemed to be repeating itself. Another Christian army was on the march towards the towns of Palestine. The Turkish propaganda was all too easy to believe. 'The British will show no mercy. They will fire on the towns and kill the civilians.' Although the people of Haifa and Acre distrusted the Turkish authorities, they also developed a profound fear of the British army.

One day, when the sea was unusually calm and the sun bright, some rocks far out from the shore became visible. Believing the rocks to be warships, the people of Acre fled in panic.

When an enemy warship did draw close to the coastline, many thought that the end had finally come. The population cowered as incoming shells screamed towards the land. But the bombardment was only intended to cut the railway between Acre and Haifa.[1]

The people of Haifa saw the power of modern artillery

demonstrated on another occasion. In 1915 the German Consul desecrated some French war graves dating from the Napoleonic period. Having heard about the event, the French navy landed an officer, who curtly delivered a letter to the German authorities before returning to his warship. The letter gave notice that, in reprisal for such disrespect, the German Consulate building would be bombarded that day at 3:00 p.m. The Consul obviously took the threat seriously because he packed up his archives and valuables and left the building. The bombardment began exactly on schedule. The first shell shrieked through the air and scored a direct hit. A couple more were enough to reduce the building to a heap of smouldering rubble. The French navy clearly wanted to make a point because they did not stop until 15 shells had been fired. None of the surrounding properties were touched.[2]

One of 'Abdu'l-Bahá's daughters recalled her father gathering some of the Bahá'ís during one of the bombardments of Haifa. He then told them 'such enchanting stories that we forgot the guns'.[3]

In the end, the atmosphere of fear and panic was too much and 'Abdu'l-Bahá decided to send the small Bahá'í community to the Druse village of Abú-Sinán, in the foothills of Galilee. Quarters were found for them in the homes of the villagers. During this time the Bahá'í leader stayed in Acre with one attendant but occasionally spent one or two nights in the village.

'Abdu'l-Bahá had often spoken of the importance of agriculture, pointing out that it is 'the fundamental basis of the community'.[4] He had, over many years before the war, purchased parcels of land near Haifa as well as in the Jordan valley. Groups of Bahá'ís moved to this land and set up as farmers. Through hard work they managed to fulfil their own needs and then produce a surplus.

Even before returning to Palestine from the West, 'Abdu'l-Bahá had sent instructions to these farming communities to renovate the derelict Roman storage pits of the area. He also instructed them how to farm so as to produce a great surplus of corn.[5]

At first this must have been relatively easy. Under Turkish rule corruption was widespread, but, for the most part, people were allowed to get on with their lives.

The situation deteriorated rapidly when Turkey entered the war on the side of the Central Powers. The British and French navies took up position to blockade the Mediterranean and the economy began to collapse.

The spring of 1915 saw signs of a good food crop and hopes were raised that starvation might be avoided. But on 12 May a heat wave struck – the worst in 35 years. In a matter of weeks, the harvest was all but destroyed.[6]

The people of Palestine were literally starving, eating grass in the fields, rummaging in the gutters for refuse. Many of the elderly and the young died. Hunger forced thousands of young women and girls into lives of prostitution.[7] Disease and malnutrition were everywhere. Bodies lay beside the main roads.

Relief supplies were offered by the United States but the German government encouraged the Turkish authorities to refuse them – lest the world should realize the Ottoman government's lack of organization.[8]

At the outbreak of war, two ships were in Haifa harbour unloading coal. This supplied local needs for a short time. After the coal was used up, the shortage of fuel was drastic. By July 1915 olive trees over a hundred years old in the

Carmel district had been cut to fuel the steam trains.[9]

Nothing could be obtained from abroad. Foreign markets were closed so the oranges were left to rot on the trees. Petrol, rice, sugar and many other basic commodities were in short supply. Even matches became unobtainable and the people had to go back to using flint and steel to light their fires.[10]

When Djemal Pasha arrived on the scene, he was aware of the danger of upsetting the local people, particularly the Arabs. 'The first order I issued on my arrival', he recalled, 'was that nothing should be taken by way of requisition from the civil population of Syria and Palestine in the 4th Army area. Prompt cash was to be paid for everything of any description whatever – food, equipment or clothing.'[11]

That this order was so flagrantly ignored tells us much about Djemal Pasha's priorities and the nature of the men under his command. With the army in control, no one in Palestine was safe. All men between the ages of 19 and 45 were drafted. Animals, grain and forage were taken away with no compensation or thought to the necessity of maintaining the infrastructure as a base of supply.[12]

Wanting to build defences and finding they were running short of supplies, the soldiers visited the farms and took great quantities of barbed wire.

Unfortunately, with the barbed wire gone, marauding Bedouin Arabs were free to raid as they wished.[13] They would descend upon the villages, steal everything they could find, carrying off not only corn and oil, but furniture, clothes, even the doors and agricultural tools, as well as driving off the cattle and horses.

Women and children fleeing raids on the Bahá'í farms would travel by wagon to Haifa to seek protection from

'Abdu'l-Bahá. On at least one occasion the Bahá'í leader
managed to have some influential members of these tribes
arrested. Much to their amazement they were forced to
restore to the poor villagers at least part of the stolen
property.[14]

Even for the army, much of the requisitioning proved
inefficient. Camels were needed for the attack on the Suez
Canal. Djemal Pasha set to work to acquire them and was
clearly proud of his achievement. 'I will merely remark
that I alone knew the greatness of the difficulties I had to
overcome to procure within a month fourteen thousand
camels, including reserves. Yet ultimately I succeeded . . .'[15]

The finest camels were taken from all over the country.
Having been driven south as far as Beersheba, huge
numbers of them died from starvation – simply because
insufficient feed had been brought along. Their carcasses
dotted the sand in all directions around the town. Others
became so weak that they had to be returned to their
owners so that they could be fattened up and rested before
being requisitioned again.[16]

Soldiers also raided the medical establishments of
Palestine, taking whatever they could find with which to
equip the army field hospitals. They clearly knew nothing
of medicine. When some of the boxes were opened, after
having been transported all the way south to Beersheba,
they were found to contain gynaecological instruments.

Food prices shot up, tripling in a single year. The cost of
transport rose similarly, owing to a lack of camels. Large
numbers of people were plunged into poverty. It was then
that the foresight of 'Abdu'l-Bahá became apparent. In
failing health He worked, travelling back and forth
between the farms, Acre and Haifa to ensure the food was

harvested, stored and distributed among the poor.

As well as distributing food, 'Abdu'l-Bahá started a dispensary with a qualified doctor in one of the villages. He also arranged for the schooling of many children.

Although born into a wealthy family, 'Abdu'l-Bahá had personally experienced years of deprivation. He had, from the age of nine, shared banishment and long periods of prison life with the rest of the family, often experiencing desperate need. His particular understanding of poverty would certainly have been made more profound by this early experience.

For 'Abdu'l-Bahá, poverty was not just a social issue but also a personal condition. In America, He had often been seen giving gifts to the poor. Very early one morning in 1912 a lady had observed 'Abdu'l-Bahá through her hotel window. The Bahá'í leader, dressed in a long oriental robe, was busy dictating letters to a secretary as He paced outside the inn.

The lady watched as a poor and wretchedly clothed man walked past the hotel. 'Abdu'l-Bahá immediately broke off the dictation and sent the secretary to bring the ragged individual back.

When they came face to face, 'Abdu'l-Bahá took the man's hand, greeting him as a welcome friend. They talked for a few moments. 'Abdu'l-Bahá smiled and soon even the ragged man managed a trace of a smile. At last, 'Abdu'l-Bahá surveyed the pitiable figure whose trousers were particularly dirty and tattered, barely serving to cover his legs.

The Bahá'í leader stepped into the shadow of the porch, laughing gently. He fumbled under the long robe, returning a moment later with trousers in hand and robe tightly gathered. He handed the trousers to the ragged man. With a parting benediction of 'May God go with you', 'Abdu'l-Bahá returned to the secretary and continued the dictation as if nothing had happened.[17]

As if the man-made chaos and misery of war were not enough, a new plague arrived in Palestine. Huge clouds of locusts swept in from the Sudan. This kind of 'wandering' locust had not been seen in the Holy Land for 40 years. The swarms were so dense and black that they obscured the sun. They arrived full grown and ready for breeding. The ground was covered in females digging in the soil and laying eggs. Not a foot of earth was free of them.

Even the military authorities became worried. If there was famine in the land, the army would suffer with everyone else. The Turks put some thousand Arab soldiers to work fighting the plague. Under the instruction of a Jewish agricultural expert, they dug trenches into which were driven the hatching insects. They knew that as soon as the young ones got their wings it would be too late to do anything.

Between the Jews and Arabs there was a wide cultural gulf. The Jews regarded the plague as something to be fought and overcome; the Arabs took it as the inevitable Will of God to which they must submit. In the end, the task was hopeless and the locusts broke in great waves over the countryside, destroying everything. Not only were green plants devoured but also the flesh of dead animals and even sleeping children.

Farmers watched the work of decades being destroyed: the very bark of the trees was chewed away, leaving dead wood, bleached like skeletons.[18]

7

Deception

No, the hand of Yahweh is not too short to save,
nor His ear too dull to hear.
But your iniquities have made a gulf
Between you and your God.

Your sins have made Him veil His face
so as not to hear you,
since your hands are stained with blood,
your fingers with crime,
your lips utter lies,
your tongues murmur treachery.

No one makes just accusations
or pleads sincerely.
All rely on nothingness, utter falsehood,
conceive harm and give birth to misery.

Isaiah 59:1–4

Captain Richard Meinertzhagen, 39 years of age, although looking younger, became head of British Field Intelligence in Egypt and Palestine just a few weeks before Allenby arrived in Cairo. He was a tall and powerful man who treated truth and falsehood as commodities, a man who delighted in mischief. He possessed an active mind, was at

ease with the unconventional and was unhampered by
doubt or habit. He listed among his interests silence, soli-
tude and space.

Meinertzhagen is a Dutch name. As well as being difficult to pronounce, it sounded far too German for comfort.
As a result, friends called him Meiner.

In Egypt Meiner found he was up against a strong
Turkish spy network. As for the British: 'At advanced headquarters', Meiner recalled, 'security arrangements were
nil.'[1] With things as they were, the British would be unable
to spring any surprises on the Turkish army.

The first thing Meiner did was to trigger a spy hunting
fever by placing the British troops on high alert. Off-duty
soldiers in the desert were often bored and probably wel-
comed the chance of some excitement. They chased and
arrested anyone they thought suspicious. In practice this
led to the harassment of anyone in Arab dress and many
innocent people were questioned before being released. It
was not long before Meiner got a taste of his own medicine. He was arrested by a zealous patrol and had to establish his identity before they would let him go.

As well as irritating the local population, Meiner's
crackdown did catch some genuine spies. A few were Arabs
employed by the Turks and others were Turks in disguise.
By questioning these, Meiner managed to learn the name
of the man at the centre of the Turkish spy network, a well-
educated Arab who lived in the town of Beersheba.

The obvious next step would have been to assassinate
the man, but Beersheba was safely inside Turkish territory
and, in any case, Meiner thought he had a better way.

A messenger was found – a man willing to cross the
front lines. Meiner gave him a package to take to the spy

master in Beersheba. The messenger, being particularly incompetent, was easily intercepted and the package quickly fell into the hands of the Turkish army. On opening it, they discovered a letter of thanks for work well done, together with a large sum in cash. The spy master was arrested and shot – without even being questioned. With their spy master assumed to have been a double agent, the entire Turkish espionage network must have been thrown into confusion and doubt.

The spy network Meiner inherited operated well enough but only far behind the Turkish front lines. He received very little information from the front itself.

By the time Allenby arrived in July 1917, Meiner had collected some 30 agents – Jews, Arabs and Egyptians – and trained them in his own special methods.

Traditionally, spies watched, listened and picked up hearsay news. Meiner disliked this kind of information, regarding it as unreliable. He preferred written evidence. At the time there were no paper shredders, so Meiner trained his agents to search for discarded documents on waste-dumps and such places. This was a new technique.

The blockade had given rise to many shortages behind Turkish lines. Food was usually scarce – so, occasionally, was ammunition. But the shortage of toilet paper was chronic. In those conditions, it must have seemed unforgivable to burn paper – irrespective of what was written on it. Thus Meiner found the cesspits to be a prolific source of discarded official documents. Though the work of recovering them was extremely unpleasant, they provided much reliable information about the activities of the Turkish army.

Both sides in Palestine did all they could to suppress the free flow of information, fearing that any snippet might be useful to their enemies. Thus harsh censorship was considered mild and a complete news blackout was usual.

After September 1916 it had become impossible for the ordinary people of Haifa to communicate with the outside world.[2] In the absence of real news, misinformation and propaganda circulated freely. This situation was particularly distressing for the Bahá'ís. 'Abdu'l-Bahá, the head of the Faith, was cut off from the large Bahá'í communities in such far-flung locations as North America, Persia, Europe and India.

There was no obvious way of getting a message out. British and French warships were blockading the Mediterranean to the west. To the south was the front line, bristling with guns and troops. To the east was the almost impassable desert of the Arabian peninsula. The only possible route was northwards overland out of Palestine then east all the way to neutral Persia, from where news could be distributed to the rest of the Bahá'í world community. Even this option was hazardous in the extreme. It would need a messenger of great skill and daring to get past hundreds of miles of military patrols and lawless bandit country. The enterprise invited death.

Yet one man did come forward to offer his services. He was an Arab called Ḥájí Ramaḍán, 75 years old and nearly blind. 'Who would suspect me?' he asked.

'Abdu'l-Bahá accepted the offer and the aged man set off, a letter carefully hidden among his few possessions. He walked for 45 days without being stopped, arriving safely in Tehran to deliver the news. The Bahá'í community was overjoyed to hear that 'Abdu'l-Bahá was still safe.

After a period of rest, the ageing messenger set out on the return journey, which proved even more difficult. Letters were sewn inside the lining of his clothes and gifts of gold he concealed in the bottom of his bags. He walked through Kermanshah and Baghdad disguised as a peddlar. Then, having acquired some boric acid lotion, he passed himself off as an eye doctor among the wild Arabs.

There was little time for rest owing to the constant risk of discovery. Despite the burden of his age and fatigue, Ḥájí Ramaḍán persisted, eventually arriving back in Haifa in safety. He then laid the gold and letters entrusted to him at the feet of 'Abdu'l-Bahá.

'Abdu'l-Bahá embraced him saying, 'Behold by what poor and humble children of God are great events served.'

After a further period of rest, this intrepid old man set out on a second mission. This time he did not reach his destination, nor did he ever return. To this day his fate remains unknown.[3]

Even though cut off from the Bahá'í world community, 'Abdu'l-Bahá was kept extremely busy caring for the needy in and around Haifa. In this work it was necessary for some things to remain secret, for example, the location of the grain secreted in old Roman storage pits.[4] The Turkish army would have been more than happy to sequester such a supply.[5]

Secrecy is one thing, spreading falsehoods is quite another. In that way, 'Abdu'l-Bahá would never be like the competing spy masters. 'If a man were to perform every good work,' wrote the Bahá'í leader, 'yet fail in the least scruple to be entirely trustworthy and honest, his good works would become as dry tinder and his failure as a soul-consuming fire.'[6]

But war, as 'Abdu'l-Bahá observed, can turn the perception of morality upside down.

> A man who kills another man is punished by execution, but a military genius who kills one hundred thousand of his fellow creatures is immortalized as a hero. One man steals a small sum of money and is imprisoned as a thief. Another pillages a whole country and is honoured as a patriot and conqueror. A single falsehood brings reproach and censure, but the wiles of politicians and diplomats excite the admiration and praise of a nation.[7]

In the secret war of espionage, deception is piled on deception, lie on lie. This makes it difficult, after the lapse of so many years, to know exactly what happened. Even with the aid of eyewitness accounts, some of the most extraordinary events can only be pieced together by guesswork. One such story concerns the highly successful German agent known as 'Franks'.[8]

The activities of Franks behind the British lines were so audacious and frequent that stories had begun to circulate about him. They even reached the British army, where they were whispered as dark rumours.

Franks, quick-witted and with a knack for languages, was able to disguise himself in several different ways. He usually crossed the front lines dressed as an Australian soldier. Most British soldiers were unfamiliar with the details of the various colonial uniforms and accents, so the deception was relatively easy.

Although British intelligence did not believe the rumours, it began to use the name 'Franks' as a kind of bogey man – to keep the front line troops on their toes. This made work much more hazardous for Franks, as the

British soldiers were less happy to accept the stories of strangers.

Doubtless, Franks's skill as a horseman enabled him to get out of many tight situations but the day came when his luck ran out and he found his escape route blocked. There was nothing for it but to put his emergency plan into operation. If he were caught dressed as an Australian soldier, he would certainly be shot as a spy. Quickly, he threw off the uniform and made other changes to his clothes.

When the British arrived, he advanced towards them, hands raised. In broken English, he explained that he was a Greek serving with the Turkish army and wished to desert. He was taken under guard and transported back to a prison camp in Egypt.

In the prison camp he must have been amused to hear some of the exaggerated stories of his own activities and the way in which the British army appeared to be searching for him. He also learned that the British spy-master, Captain Meinertzhagen, was coming to inspect the camp. This is when Franks must have devised his plan of escape.

He contacted the guards and told them that he had information which Meiner would want to hear for himself – and that he would give it to no one else. Still posing as a Greek, he told Meiner that he had worked directly with Franks and could provide information about him. Meiner was interested, though suspicious.

Franks was taken to the Greek Consul in Cairo for questioning. Having lived in Greece for several years, Franks was able to pass himself off as a native. He described the parts of Greece he knew well and at last the Consul pronounced him genuine.

With escape achieved, Franks turned to the question of

revenge. It was Meiner who had managed to put the British troops on high alert. It was Meiner who had been the cause of his downfall.

Even though in the lion's den, his identity was still unknown and Franks felt himself to be in a position of strength. He conceived a trap, baited with something that Meiner would never be able to resist. 'I can lead you to Franks himself.'

Meiner listened to the plan and then agreed. Franks was taken back to no man's land and released.

Two weeks later Franks rode his horse into a deserted wadi. It was five miles from the sea and three miles inside the British lines: a lonely spot, almost romantic. He had arrived well before 4:00 p.m. – early for his pre-arranged meeting with Meiner. His assistant, perhaps the only person on the Turkish or British sides that Franks felt he could really trust, would arrive in the wadi two hours later. The shadows would be long by then and the deception would work more easily.

Meiner arrived in the wadi on time, coming alone as had been agreed. Still posing as the Greek, Franks showed Meiner some documents which he claimed had come from the famed German agent. Meiner looked at the documents and liked what he saw.

Franks began to relate a carefully prepared story. He told Meiner that the German agent was on his way but was bringing an orderly with him. This would make capture more difficult.

'Are you armed?' Franks asked.

'What do you think?'

Meiner was keeping one hand in a pocket all the time. Franks could guess what he was holding there.

As the shadows began to fill the wadi, Franks's assistant appeared, dressed in an Australian uniform and riding a horse.

'That's the orderly,' Franks explained, riding over to greet the newcomer. The 'orderly' handed over some documents and said that Franks had been chased back to the Turkish lines by British soldiers.

The story seemed convincing but Meiner was still suspicious. He cautiously led his horse away a few yards before removing his hand from the gun pocket to mount.

That was when the shooting started. In the fading light Franks and his assistant shot and missed. Meiner emptied his revolver, missing Franks, who managed to ride away, but hitting the assistant, who fell to the ground with a shrill scream.

If the light in the wadi had been better, Meiner might have guessed the truth earlier. It was only on coming close to the wounded spy that he discovered he had shot and mortally wounded a woman. She died within a few minutes.

Confused and strangely ashamed, Meiner did not know what to do. After a few minutes he decided not to report the event. Instead he kicked a hole in the bed of the gully and buried the body in a shallow grave.

Some months later, when Jaffa was captured by the British army, Meiner was given the task of searching through the buildings of the town for important papers. At last he discovered the house where Franks had been living, and in it, a picture of the famous German agent himself, together with his wife. It was only then that Meiner knew the identity of the strange Greek prisoner-of-war and of the woman who had died in the lonely wadi.

8

The Battle for Gaza

I saw an angel standing in the sun, and he shouted aloud to all the birds that were flying high overhead in the sky, 'Come here. Gather together at the great feast that God is giving. There will be the flesh of kings for you, and the flesh of great generals and heroes, the flesh of horses and their riders and of all kinds of men, citizens and slaves, small and great.

Revelation 19:17–18

A pile of paperwork was waiting for Allenby when he marched into General Headquarters, Cairo, in June 1917. He glanced at one or two and, finding them to be routine, swept the whole lot off the desk and onto the floor. From then on, such matters would be dealt with by junior staff officers. He promptly set off to view the troops and their conditions at first hand. The staff at headquarters did not see him for several days.

Unannounced visits to the front line were Allenby's speciality. It made the officers distinctly uneasy when 'the Bull' was out and about. On one visit Allenby noticed a signalman waving flags to send a hurried message back to divisional headquarters. Always inquisitive, the general approached the soldier.

'What are you doing?' he asked.

'Signalling, sir,' the young soldier replied, evasively.

'I can see that, but for what reason are you signalling?'

'A warning that you are approaching Divisional Headquarters, sir.'

'Oh, and what form is the message taking?'

The signalman blushed. 'Please, sir, "B.B.L."'

'"B.B.L"? What does that mean?'

'Please, sir, "Bloody Bull's Loose!"'[1]

Most officers commanded through detailed orders and a rigid hierarchy. Unquestioning obedience was considered the most praiseworthy of qualities. Allenby was different. He would explain the problem to his subordinates then finish by saying, 'These are merely general orders; don't be tied to any definite line; carry out the work in the way that seems best.'[2]

Freedom of action made some officers feel distinctly uneasy. 'I was just following orders' was no longer going to be an adequate excuse when things went wrong. The more adventurous, however, found it exhilarating. The more traditional put in for transfers to other fronts. Thus, after a short time, Allenby was left with a dynamic and innovative team.

A new spirit was in the air. Orders started to flow from GHQ Cairo relaxing some regulations and making sure that others were strictly enforced.[3] In the past officers had been forbidden from dining in public in anything other than breeches, field boots and spurs. This rule, deeply resented in the stifling heat of summer, was overturned. On the other hand, cavalry were forbidden to wear short trousers and were instructed to use their chin-straps properly – these regulations Allenby considered important for maintaining the fighting efficiency of his men.

Another boost for the men came when soldiers were permitted to dance with the VAD nurses. Morale improved. Drunkenness and petty crime decreased. The number of desertions, which before Allenby's arrival had been rising, started to fall.

'There is a wonderful sense of optimism over the arrival of the new general, Allenby,' observed one Australian cavalryman. 'He has come right out to the line. We hear that he is a cavalry man too.'[4]

If the front line troops approved of a general who would come close to the fighting, the staff officers may not have been so sure. Within a few weeks, headquarters were transferred from the pleasant environment of Cairo to an uncomfortable and none too safe position just behind the front line, on the very edge of Palestine.

Amid the chaos of the move, a liaison officer working with the desert Arabs reported in. He was 29 years old, with a weather-beaten face that gave him the appearance of being older than his years. His short thin body concealed an extremely strong and wiry frame. His most striking features were blue, deep-set eyes and a determined, purposeful expression. This unusual appearance was enhanced by the fact that he wore Arab dress, from headgear to bare feet.

When Meinertzhagen met this strange little man he asked, 'Boy or girl?'

The man smiled and blushed, saying, 'Boy.'[5]

This was Captain T. E. Lawrence, later to be known as Lawrence of Arabia. In spite of holding no official power, Lawrence had persuaded the Arabs to mount an attack on the Turks, first crossing miles of waterless desert, then capturing the port of Aqaba on the Red Sea.

Allenby, tall, broad and sharply turned out in regulation

uniform, looked to be the very opposite of Lawrence. Not only were his strict views on uniform famous throughout the army, so was his temper. Instead of looking directly at the man before him, as was Allenby's usual custom, he looked sideways, puzzled.

Unabashed, Lawrence explained that he had not had time to change before meeting the general. He then proceeded to ask for two hundred thousand gold sovereigns as well as stores and weapons for the Arabs. Using a map, he explained his ideas. Allenby did not talk much nor ask many questions but listened to Lawrence's plan.

One of the principal military supply routes for the Turks was a single track railway which linked Turkey in the north with Medina and Mecca far to the south. This line, the Hejaz railway, skirted the Arabian Desert down the length of Palestine and was vulnerable to attack. Lawrence, who had a profound knowledge of Islam, knew that this was more than a supply line. Its religious significance was such that the Turks would be forced to keep it running – at any cost. A large number of Turkish troops would be needed to defend it from the desert Arabs.

'Well,' said Allenby, at last, 'I will do for you what I can.' And so he did.[6] The Arab forces may have made little difference to the balance of power between the two sides but they occasionally cut the line, made the supply position uncertain and did much to sap the morale of the Turkish forces.

One of Allenby's first big decisions was how and where to attack the Turkish lines.

Gaza had been attacked twice already, each mission ending in disaster. Before the second of these attacks the

Turks intercepted a coded radio message which they managed to decipher. It said that an English infantry force would be landed from the sea behind Turkish lines so that Gaza could be attacked from the rear. The Turks, believing the message to be a ruse, continued to prepare for an attack from the front. They were correct.[7] The attack was repelled – but only just.

The British attacks on Gaza had failed but the front between Gaza and Beersheba looked even less promising. Inland from the coast, water was very scarce. The prospect of moving an army through the area and engaging in a protracted battle was a logistical nightmare. This was a truth not lost on Djemal Pasha. '. . . as long as we were holding these defences', he observed, 'the English were compelled to remain in the desert, while we were in a region which could be described as cultivated.'[8]

A third possibility for Allenby was to attack Beersheba itself, hoping to take the town so quickly that the retreating Turks would have no time to destroy the wells.

Whichever plan was adopted, secrecy would be of the utmost importance. Fresh Turkish troops were crossing the Euphrates and streaming south into Palestine. If news of Allenby's attack plan leaked out, the reinforcements would be concentrated on his target area and the endeavour would be doomed. The general called for Meiner, his spy chief, to come to see him. Together they agreed on a series of 'camouflage' methods by which the Turks could be deceived.

For the entire period of preparation the bulk of the British troops were to be kept opposite the place they were not going to attack. Then, at the last moment, they were to move rapidly and secretly to the real target. The railway line and water pipeline used to support the attack would not be extended until the very last moment. Supply dumps would be made so as to take up as little room as possible and would be built up very quickly so that the Turkish spies would not be able to guess how much food and ammunition they contained. Much of the equipment would be moved under cover of darkness and concealed in the sand.[9]

A series of other standard deceptions were put in place. Near the target area, radio communication was used as little as possible. Conversely, in other places radio traffic was boosted. Dummy messages were sent in codes which the Turks were thought to have cracked. Genuine messages were carried by hand as far as possible.

Meiner had radio receiving stations installed to listen to the Turkish communications – including one on the top of the Great Pyramid. If the British deception failed, it would be vital to know as soon as possible.

The activities of Meiner had made intelligence gathering difficult for the Turkish army. But it was not without opportunities. The front line troops were always on the lookout and, on at least two occasions in the autumn of 1917, they had come close to capturing British officers carrying vital documents.

Then, on 10 October, a British cavalry officer was seen near Turkish lines. There was an exchange of fire. The British officer escaped but dropped some of his belongings in the process. When the Turkish soldiers arrived at the scene, they found the officer's rifle, water bottle, sandwiches and field glasses, as well as a bloodstained knapsack.

The knapsack was sent back to Turkish intelligence for evaluation. It was found to contain the substantial sum of

20 pounds in notes and a number of sensitive documents. The man who had been carrying the knapsack was dressed in the uniform of an intelligence officer, an identity supported by the papers in his bag.

Nothing was spelled out but the implication was clear. The problems of water supply inland were too great. Only minor operations could be carried out against Beersheba. This left Gaza as the only possible target for the British offensive.

There was also a letter which looked as if it had been carried in the knapsack for some time – perhaps a precious link with family back in England. The sentiments and the writing were judged to be from the hand of a woman.

63 Bedford Gardens,
LONDON, S.W.

August 21st, 1917

Dearest,

How I wish you were here now!

I am simply longing for you and would love to show you our dear little baby son.

I am so proud of him! He is such a splendid little fellow and so good.

You must not worry about either of us, as I get stronger every day, and baby, the doctor says, could not be better.

Richard is the name we are giving him – I know it is the one you always had in mind, and I chose it, as I felt you would be glad I had remembered it.

All your sisters came and saw him and Alice wanted to adopt him at once.

I sent you a telegram as soon as baby was born, and

your reply arrived three days later. If it had been you arriving instead of the telegram, how lovely it would have been. Darling, you must try and come soon to see your little son. Don't smile if I say he already has a look of you. He is such a darling and you will love him so.

I heard the last raid, but no bombs were thrown anywhere near. Poor baby! Fancy coming into the world to find this awful war going on and Germans dropping bombs all over London. Louis had a narrow escape in the office, for some of his windows were broken.

Good-bye, my darling! – Nurse says I must not tire myself by writing too much – so no more now but I will write again soon and then it will be a longer letter than this. Take care of your precious self! All my love and many kisses.

Your loving wife,

Mary

Baby sends a kiss to Daddy.[10]

In the days following the find British troops were very active in the area, searching for the officer's lost bag. A furious message was sent back to GHQ demanding that inexperienced officers not be used on reconnaissance missions in the future. There were also demands that the officer responsible for the loss should be court martialed.

Turkish intelligence was sceptical about the find. It was too good to be believed. The Germans found it altogether more convincing. The package looked correct. It contained the sort of things that an officer would be carrying to avoid them being stolen. The reaction of the British troops to the loss looked just too genuine to be a fake. In the end the German view won over.

Fresh Turkish troops were sent to reinforce Gaza ready for the expected attack. Sure enough, a heavy British bombardment of Gaza began on 27 October.

Three days later, under cover of darkness, British troops started marching from their camps towards the site of the forthcoming battle. For one cavalry officer, Lieutenant Wilson, it was a 30-mile moonlit march. And only then the attack could begin. He charged, with the others, through shell and machine gun fire, across an open plain. Then, with sword and gun, he continued through two Turkish defence systems, arriving at the wells of Beersheba as they were being prepared for demolition.

Turkish troops defending Beersheba reported the attack as it started and requested reinforcements. The high command refused. They 'knew' it must be a diversionary tactic. The main British assault would surely be on Gaza.

In the days that followed Lieutenant Wilson wrote home of his adventures. 'Just a few lines to let you know that I am quite well and very happy despite the recent battlings which to say the least has been rather strenuous. You will see by the address that we have taken Beersheba, it was a great show, we galloped it from behind whilst the Infantry came at the front.'[11]

For Allenby, the deception was a triumph, for most of the wells of Beersheba had been taken intact. The officer who had dropped the precious knapsack had been none other than Meinertzhagen himself and the love letter had been constructed by his sister, Mary.

Meiner had one other game to play in the following days. In this he acted alone, against the instructions of his Commander-in-Chief, who considered the idea beyond the pale.

In the propaganda war it was standard practice for British aeroplanes to drop leaflets over Turkish held towns. Information was hard to get hold of, so people eagerly picked the leaflets up to read. The Turkish authorities responded by threatening the death penalty for anyone caught in possession of the enemy propaganda.[12]

Turkish soldiers arriving to defend Gaza from the expected attack found that British aeroplanes were dropping packets of cigarettes wrapped in propaganda leaflets. Such gifts must have been hard to resist, whatever the penalty. Tobacco was in short supply. Finding the cigarettes to be good, the soldiers would have quickly developed the habit of looking out for the British aeroplanes.

Then came news that Beersheba had fallen. Gaza was in danger of being cut off. With morale low, the cigarettes must have been especially welcome. We can imagine soldiers smoking to pass the tedious hours of guard duty. But the final drop of cigarettes was not quite the same.

Five days after Beersheba fell, Gaza was attacked. The Turkish defence proved feeble, some of the front line troops surrendering almost without a fight. They were found to be in a somewhat dazed state. It was almost as if they had been smoking opium.

9

The Waters of the Nile

*And out came another horse, bright red, and its rider was given this
duty: to take away peace from the earth and set people killing each
other. He was given a huge sword.*

Revelation 6:4

Even with all their differences, there is one strange similarity in the way 'Abdu'l-Bahá and General Allenby were
regarded: both were hailed as prophets of God and both
denied it emphatically.

There was a tradition current in Palestine at the turn of
the 19th century – it could have been called a prophecy.
Attributed to the 10th century poet Ibn Khasri, it ran as
follows: 'The man who will conquer Jerusalem and redeem
it from the infidel for all time to come will enter the Holy
City humbly on foot and his name is God's Prophet.'[1]

There were other versions of this tradition then
current. It was said that the Turks would hold on to
Jerusalem until 'a Prophet of the Lord brought the waters
of the Nile to Palestine'.[2]

A powerful prophet indeed might be needed to achieve
this. The Nile was well over 150 miles from the Palestinian
border. Between them lay hills, valleys and desert, not to
mention the salt water of the Suez canal. For much of the

journey the flow of water would need to be uphill.

By 1885 the prophet's task had been made somewhat easier by the construction of a sweet-water canal between the Nile and Port Said at the north end of the Suez canal. By 1916 a filtration works had been constructed to clean this water. It was then pumped along pipes running under the Suez canal to be stored in masonry reservoirs on the other side. Thus 600,000 gallons of Nile water a day were pumped across the canal to within 150 miles of the Palestinian border.

One barrier had been passed but the water still had to cross a wide expanse of desert if it was to fulfil the prophecy. This was the barren land through which Moses and the Israelites were supposed to have wandered for 40 years before reaching their goal.

This was the land across which the British army was intending to advance. It had been calculated that a soldier could manage on less than a gallon of water a day and that a horse could go without a drink for up to 48 hours. But even at that subsistence level sufficient water was not available from the local wells. The generals could not, like Moses, strike the rock and have water pour out of the ground.[3]

'We were on the Arabian desert,' recalled one Welsh soldier,

> . . . seeing nothing but sand; eating sand with every morsel of food; inhaling sand with each breath; our eyes were full of sand, making them smart like red hot coals; ears and nostrils bunged with sand . . .
>
> I made a vow then, that if ever I got home from this, and if anybody asked me to come to Swansea Bay for a day on the sands, I would shoot him.[4]

Large numbers of Egyptian labourers were employed to assemble and bury 147 miles of steel water pipe. The Suez canal had been largely dug by forced labour but this work, hard and unpleasant though it was, was done by paid Egyptian labourers. The money seemed good and many poor families were delighted to have an income.

The head of the pipeline was always just behind the advancing troops. From there the water was carried to the troops in tanks pulled by teams of camels. When the battle front moved forward, another stretch of pipeline would be laid.

But for men marching through the fierce heat, there would never be enough water. 'Everything I ate was warm and sticky, and covered with swarms of flies,' the Welsh trooper lamented. 'It was impossible to place anything in your mouth without having a mouthful of flies as well. We couldn't have a spoonful of cold water for our parched lips and burning throats. Our lips were cracked and bleeding, therefore attracting more flies, if that was possible.'[5]

By the time Allenby took control of the operation, all that remained was to extend the pipeline for a few miles for it to reach the border. With the capture of Beersheba in November 1917, the British had arrived in Palestine. It would take time for the pipeline to catch up with the army but at that time of the year the weather was more favourable and the local wells might be expected to suffice.

Of the 17 wells in Beersheba, two had been completely demolished and two partly damaged by the retreating Turkish army. Several of the others were concealed in buildings and were not discovered for a number of days.

With troops pouring into the town, the weather suddenly changed. The following days were the hottest of the

year. An arid wind blew in from the desert, covering everything in fine dust.

Conditions became so bad that severe water rationing
was imposed. With people this was easy enough to enforce.
Even the camels proved biddable, for they would naturally
drink in two bouts and could be led away after the first
session before they had drunk their fill. It was not so easy
with the horses. Scenting water, the desperate animals
became uncontrollable. Many broke free and charged the
watering troughs, not letting up until they had satisfied
their thirst. It was only the stout guard rails around the
troughs that stopped the wholesale destruction of the
watering area.

Over the following days new wells were found and
pumping machinery repaired. At last the advancing
pipeline reached Beersheba. The waters of the Nile had
arrived in Palestine.

Soon Allenby was widely believed to be the expected
prophet – not just in Palestine but in Egypt also. His fame
might have been useful. How much better would be his
reception by the local people if he were regarded as some
kind of warlike Messiah – certainly better than if he were
seen as an invading foreign general. Yet Allenby would
have nothing of it. He was genuinely free of such preten-
sions. He was also a deeply religious man and the idea
must have been an anathema to him. But, however much
he denied it, the rumour persisted.

The Turkish authorities also tried to stamp out the
rumour. They were not about to give in easily. They would
defend this sacred part of their ancient empire to the last.

Still, the idea would not go away, even in the minds of
the Turkish soldiers. Some of the more superstitious even

believed that the general was possessed of magical powers. On one occasion Allenby was inspecting a group of prisoners by the side of the road. He smiled and asked a few questions before moving on. One group of Turks, who had been cowering in abject fear whilst he was passing, quickly admitted that they had been planning an escape. They firmly believed that Allenby could read their minds and wished to have the blame fall only on the originator of the escape plan.[6]

Every victory Allenby's men scored and every mile they drew closer to the Holy City must have reinforced the impression. Perhaps the prophecy was self-fulfilling. It weakened Turkish morale and made it easier for Allenby's army to win the battle. No man can fight at his best when he believes that fate is set against him.

It is hard to imagine people believing that such a practical, worldly man as Allenby was a prophet. Yet so they did. Perhaps it was another strange coincidence which made the idea hard to resist. The word used in Arabic to describe the 'lesser' prophets, such as Elijah or Job, is 'nabí'. The Arabic word for God is 'Alláh'. Thus the general's name 'Allenby' sounds uncannily close to the Arabic phrase 'Alláh-en-nabí' – prophet of God.

After the fall of Gaza and Beersheba, Allenby urged his forces to pursue the Turkish army with ruthless determination, spurring them on to ignore fatigue, hunger and thirst.

Water difficulties again made this hard. The retreating forces not only destroyed the wells wherever they could but also the pumping equipment. Even after a well had been cleared of rubble, water often had to be raised by bucket. This made watering the horses so slow that soldiers retreating on foot could outdistance the pursuing cavalry.

Lieutenant Wilson reported seeing one soldier driven mad by thirst. The Turks were defending a well 200 yards ahead. The soldier in question stood up and started running towards the Turkish lines to ask them to give him a drink. His friends managed to pull him down to the ground before he was shot. He was sent back to base where he quickly recovered.

Lieutenant Wilson also reported on the friction he saw between the Turks and the Germans as they were pushed back towards Jerusalem – even though the two countries were in close alliance. The Turks found the Germans arrogant. The Germans thought of the Turks as savages.

Following a cavalry charge the ground was strewn with wounded, dead and dying. Wilson was supervising a German medical man who was doing his best for the wounded of both sides. The German had been looking after one casualty when, looking up, he noticed a wounded Turkish soldier covered in a cloak. The German sprang to his feet and rushed over to where the Turk lay. He snatched the coat, tossed it aside and kicked the Turk in the ribs. 'Look!' he shouted, outraged. 'A Turk covered by a German cloak.'[7]

It was a very good cloak and Wilson took it for his own use. The colonel spoke to him about it a couple of days later. 'I should take that off if I were you Bob,' he said, 'somebody might shoot you.'

The British northward advance continued rapidly. Jaffa fell on 16 November. The goal of taking Jerusalem by Christmas looked to be possible. Then, two days later, the winter rains began and water again became a threat.

Tracks that only days before had thrown up clouds of dust with the passage of a single marching man quickly became impassable quagmires.

Even when the winter rains started, drinking water was still in short supply. Early downpours quickly ran off the baked soil of the hillsides leaving only the mist as a reminder of their visit.

Having just arrived in Palestine, Tudor Pole was sent up to the front to take part in the advance on Jerusalem. He had moved to a position almost in sight of the Holy City when he was wounded and sent back to hospital in Cairo.

Jerusalem stands on a natural defensive position and looked particularly difficult to attack. Machine gun positions were set up outside the city, ready to fire on any Turks or Germans who tried to escape. Seeing that some Turkish soldiers had gone to hide in the old part of the city, the machine gunners called for the artillery to flush them out.

'No,' came the reply. 'That we cannot do. The city is holy – General Allenby's orders.'

Then, as the machine gunners watched, a big crowd of women and children emerged into the open, among them a few Turkish soldiers.

'I cannot fire on them,' protested the machine gunner.

Then a call came through from headquarters. 'What the hell is the matter with your guns . . . Why don't you fire?'

But the gunner still refused.

'Fire, man! Fire!' The order was shouted down the phone.

'These are only a few Turks . . . It will be a massacre.'

'Who the hell are you to disobey an order? Consider yourself under close arrest as soon as we have captured the Holy City.'

When the machine gunner reported in after several days of heavy fighting, he expected to be court martialed. And the penalty for disobeying a direct order would usually be death. He stood before the Brigadier. '. . . that little matter of placing you under close arrest is over,' he was told. 'You see, we all make mistakes at some time or other. That's all, sergeant.'[8]

An artillery barrage might have softened up the defences but Allenby refused to use any method of attack which risked damaging the city. The destruction of Jerusalem would at once have alienated Christians, Jews and Muslims. Allenby ordered his troops to outflank the city, threatening to cut it off entirely.

At last, on 8 December, the order came to take control of the city – but not to damage it in any way. The officer responsible was worried as to how to deal with the defending Turks. He sent back a message: 'What shall we do?'

The reply came back: 'Pray.'[9]

When British troops entered Jerusalem the following day they found it to be empty of enemy forces. The mayor came out with the keys of the city and tried to find someone to whom he could surrender them. As the soldiers were all busily engaged in military operations of various kinds, he finally surrendered to two cooks he happened to meet. The symbolic keys were then passed through various hands to a senior officer who formally accepted the surrender later.

When Allenby arrived at Jerusalem later that day, he dismounted at the gate and entered the city on foot.[10]

10

Djemal Pasha

The sixth angel emptied his bowl over the great river Euphrates; all the water dried up so that a way was made for the kings of the East to come in.

Revelation 16:12

Biyuk Djemal Pasha[1] was a small man who wore a thick black beard which emphasized his pallid complexion. When at rest he was not an impressive figure. It was only when he arose and moved that his energy revealed itself. He could uncoil like a spring and his eyes would glitter in acute, near feverish concentration.[2]

Though not described as attractive, he had a charismatic charm which helped him to win the confidence of many educated people – a confidence he often betrayed.

Energy, ambition and intelligence had projected him from humble origins into high office. He was one of the Young Turks who seized power in 1908. He then manoeuvred himself into a position of even greater influence as one of the three most powerful men in the Ottoman Empire. Although the Sultan still officially held the highest office, it was Enver Pasha, Talaat Pasha and Djemal Pasha who had the real power.[3] Djemal Pasha, in his mid-forties, was the eldest of the three. He did not always see eye to eye with the others.

Djemal Pasha's diplomatic skill was much in evidence before the war. He managed to persuade the French government to lend Turkey five hundred million *francs* to help mobilize the army. Turkey then joined the Central Powers and used this army to fight against France.

Perhaps this ruthless dedication to the interests of the Ottoman Empire helped to win him increasing influence. By early in the war he was not only head of the Turkish 4th Army and Minister of the Marine but also controlled the whole Syria-Palestine region.

It was under his orders that Turkish forces had moved south from Turkey across the River Euphrates, advancing through Palestine and across the Sinai desert to the Suez canal. Though heavily outnumbered, he had kept the British army at bay, forcing it to divert scarce resources away from the western front and thus relieving Germany, Turkey's ally. It was also under his single-minded rule that Palestine had been devastated to the point of mass starvation.

Turkey, centre of a vast and ancient empire, was ever fearful of separatist groups. Just as the Jews longed for the establishment of a modern state of Israel, many of the Arabs wanted independence from Turkey.

Djemal Pasha used an iron hand to put down the threat of subversion. It was easy for such a man to dispose of enemies within his domain, whether perceived or real. And he did not hesitate to execute those who got in his way. He was convinced that harsh punishments made Turkish rule more secure. 'I am certain', he professed, 'that to the executions in April 1916, alone do we owe the fact that there was no rising in Syria . . .'[4]

Everyone suffered under the Allied blockade and the inefficiency of Turkish military rule but it was the minority communities which were put in particular danger. The Holy Land was home not just to Muslims but also to smaller numbers of Jews, Christians, Druses and Bahá'ís. With the legal protection of minority communities effectively removed, many people took the chance to settle old scores. The predicament of the minorities worsened dramatically as the influence of Germany grew.

The Bahá'í community had its own enemies, who lost no time in stirring up trouble for 'Abdu'l-Bahá. In particular, they started rumours about a supposed anti-Turkish attitude and plots against the authorities.

The claims were taken seriously and 'Abdu'l-Bahá was investigated. There was real anxiety within the Bahá'í community. One of those waiting outside the house where 'Abdu'l-Bahá was being questioned later reported what he overheard. 'I could hear His clear commanding voice through the open window right above, talking to the Turkish commission with dignity, as if He were the investigator and they the culprit.'[5]

'Abdu'l-Bahá had experienced danger on many occasions. His attitude was always one of calm assurance and Djemal Pasha was a man who seemed to respect those who would not be intimidated.

Aaron Aaronsohn, a Jewish agricultural expert with connections in the United States, came to Djemal Pasha to complain about the misdeeds of the Turkish officers, agents and troops, and explained that the protection of agriculture was in the interests of the Turkish army. Djemal Pasha was furious.

'What would you say if I hanged you?' he asked.

'I could say nothing Excellency', Aaronsohn replied, 'but the weight of my heavy corpse would make the gallows crack so loud that the sound of it would reach America.'

After that Djemal Pasha gave Aaronsohn no more personal trouble and for a time conditions improved.[6]

When Djemal Pasha encamped close to Acre, he told the governor that he must see 'Abdu'l-Bahá immediately. Riding a donkey, 'Abdu'l-Bahá went to the military cantonment. Djemal Pasha received 'Abdu'l-Bahá courteously but then brought accusations of religious mischief-making and made a veiled threat to take action. 'Abdu'l-Bahá replied that mischief-making was of two kinds, political and religious. He pointed to the Pasha and said that so far the political mischief-maker had not caused any damage and it was to be hoped that the religious mischief-maker would not do so either.[7]

For Djemal Pasha there was mischief aplenty. In 1915 he entered into secret negotiations, offering to overthrow the Sultan and take the position himself – if only the British would supply him with arms.[8] Having their own plans for the Middle East, the British offered only to give Djemal Pasha the kingship of Syria.[9] Wisely, neither side trusted the other and, predictably, the negotiations broke down.

A further encounter between 'Abdu'l-Bahá and Djemal Pasha occurred in 1916. About seven o'clock one morning 'Abdu'l-Bahá called for a carriage to be readied and a short while later set out from Haifa towards Nazareth. His health was not very good at the time. Fatigue combined with physical weakness to make the journey very difficult. It was not until seven in the evening that the carriage arrived at a

German hotel in Nazareth where 'Abdu'l-Bahá stayed the night.

At one o'clock the next day 'Abdu'l-Bahá went to lunch with one of the notables of the town, where dining as well were Djemal Pasha and nearly two hundred of his war leaders.

As absolute ruler of Syria and Palestine, the Pasha was accustomed to people treating him with respect. He did not need to treat others with any consideration and would not usually rise from his seat for anyone.

But for three hours 'Abdu'l-Bahá spoke to the gathering in Turkish on a variety of philosophical and religious subjects. Everyone stopped eating to listen and even the Pasha became polite and deferential. When, at four o'clock, 'Abdu'l-Bahá rose to leave, it was the Pasha himself who led the Bahá'í teacher by the hand. 'Abdu'l-Bahá remained for a while in the reception room answering still more questions. He was finally accompanied out of the house and down the steps by Djemal Pasha.[10]

But the doubt sown by 'Abdu'l-Bahá's enemies at last bore fruit. Djemal Pasha made a decision and proclaimed an order that in the event of the Turkish army being forced to retreat from Haifa, 'Abdu'l-Bahá would be crucified on Mount Carmel.[11]

The Valley of Death

The future generation, your children who are to come after you, as also the stranger from a distant country, will see the plagues of that land and the diseases Yahweh will inflict on it, and will exclaim, 'Sulphur, salt, scorched earth, the whole land through! No one will sow, nothing grow, no grass spring ever again.'

Deuteronomy 29:21–3

Other matters were occupying the General Headquarters of the Eastern Expeditionary Force. The Turks had dug in along a line stretching from the coast just north of Jaffa, inland to the Judæan hills just north of Jerusalem and then down into the salty desert of the Jordan valley near the Dead Sea.

It was time for the British War Cabinet to decide whether to allow Allenby to press on northwards or to use the troops and resources for an attack on a different front. For all his successes, Allenby must have been thought too young a general to make recommendations unsupervised. Early in 1918 General Smuts was dispatched from Europe to make an assessment of the situation. After seeing the ground at first hand, he decided that Allenby's Palestine front was the best option. He then set about planning the push forward.

The plan was a joint effort – officially, though it perhaps owed more to Smuts, the senior general, than to Allenby. At such a stage, Allenby must have missed input from his reliable intelligence chief. For Meiner had recently been summoned back to London to work in the War Office. Meiner himself was 'disgusted' at the move.

The plan, when it was completed, was unsurprising. The army would push on from Jerusalem, down into the Jordan valley, cross the river and eventually reach the Hejaz railway. By this means it intended to split the Turkish army, leaving 20,000 troops isolated far to the south in Medina. Only then would the army advance north in a series of pushes, leaving enough time in between to consolidate. The objectives were Beirut (rather than the more politically significant Damascus) and then Aleppo and the Turkish border. The idea was sound, though rather stiff and somewhat mechanical.

With the plan completed, Smuts departed for England and Allenby dutifully started preparing for the attack.

Back in London, Meiner, now on the central planning staff, had access to the plan. He did not like what he saw. 'It is unsound from a military stand-point', he observed, 'and unpracticable from a shipping stand-point.'

Even with Meiner gone, the British Intelligence Service was still active. But knowledge of conditions in the Jordan valley was somewhat sketchy. One report stated: 'Nothing is known of the climate in summer-time, since no civilized human being has yet been found to spend summer there.'

Lieutenant Wilson had by now been posted to the Jordan valley. 'Even the flies died of the heat,' he recalled. But some things did survive. 'Our unpleasant companions included scorpions black and yellow, huge tarantula spiders and, even more venomous, centipedes six inches long with pincers that could inflict an almost fatal injury.'

On one occasion Wilson was leading his troops through the valley when he saw one of his trooper's horses gallop past him as fast as a racehorse. The man had let go the reins and was covering his face with his hands. They had just ridden over a hornets' nest and a whole swarm was after them. Both man and beast were covered in the angry, stinging insects. The trooper spent a long time in hospital after that and the horse lost all its hair.[1]

Few of the soldiers could have imagined the conditions they were to face in the 'Valley of Death'. The Turkish army was further north, in a more hospitable part of the valley. The Turks taunted the British with propaganda leaflets dropped from aeroplanes. Lieutenant Wilson remembered reading one. 'Flies die in July, men in August and we will come and bury you in September.'[2]

To raise their morale, the men devised various entertainments. 'One of our troopers had a fighting scorpion that lived in a cigarette tin,' Wilson reported.

It was the reigning champion, the victor of about a dozen contests. Someone else had a fighting tarantula with an equally illustrious record, and a fight was arranged between them. As soon as they found themselves in the ring – usually a cardboard box – they sensed what was expected of them but, on this occasion, both looked surprised to find themselves opposed to members of a different race. After a bit of preliminary sparring which went in favour of the scorpion – naturally more nimble on its feet than the spider . . . He sailed in to deliver his blow, which took the form of a rapid swing of his long tail over his back and head. But the spider also knew what to do. He just stood his ground then, with one nip, pinched the scor-

pion's tail in half and leisurely proceeded to devour his
foe. It was a sad trooper who threw his cigarette tin away.[3]

The climate, poisonous animals and disease proved far
more costly than the opposing army. For every one soldier
wounded or killed in action, ten fell victim to disease.[4]
Malaria was a particular problem. Allenby was probably
the first military commander in that region – in which
many armies had perished – to understand the risk of the
disease.[5] Insect nets were issued and a programme of
drainage instituted. Front line troops were changed at frequent intervals so that soldiers weakened from one attack
of malaria were not reinfected before they had regained
their strength. However, malaria is not a disease which is
easily defeated and while Allenby's forces suffered less than
the Turks and the Germans, losses were still severe.

The troops could not stay long in the valley and were
regularly rotated. During these changeovers the valley
could be left almost undefended. They were therefore
carried out under cover of darkness, and very quietly. The
paths up out of the valley were narrow and precipitous.
There were few places wide enough for two regiments to
pass. On reaching a wide area, the outgoing regiment
would stop and rest while the incoming one moved past.
When the men were roused to resume their trek, it was not
unusual to find that one or two had died from exhaustion
following their month in the valley.

Once out of the valley, Wilson was given nine days of
welcome leave in Cairo. This was a chance to sleep, eat
good food and relax – even though the Military Police were
always on hand to ensure the servicemen adhered to
uniform regulations. It was in Cairo that Wilson met an

Irish nurse. Even though he insisted on calling her 'Paddie', she seemed to like him.

Wilson described the meeting in one of his letters home:

> Met a topping little VAD . . . There was nothing much in it, but you get so fed up with soldiers' company that it's a nice change – she is an Irishman.

Shortly after, the nurse sent him a telegram to say that she would accept his offer – and so they were engaged.[6]

Gradually, more land was coming under the control of the British army. For the local people this brought some relief. Whereas the British soldiers were as likely to steal food as the Turks had been, the British authorities would at least give compensation – if the wrongdoing could be proved.

One fraud carried out by the soldiers involved the labels from tins of Tickler's marmalade.

A British army quarter master recalled being approached by one of the soldiers. 'What's your trouble, Gunner Killock?' he asked.

'Oh, no trouble at all,' the gunner said. 'I was just thinking if you could spare me a few labels.'

'Labels! and what the devil could you do with them?'

'You know the ones I mean,' the soldier persisted, 'the ones with the photo of a lemon leaf on them.'

The quarter master looked at the gunner. 'Killock,' he said, 'you go into your dugout and rest. You have been out in the sun too long.'

'No really,' the man protested. 'I'll tell you what I will do. For every label of Tickler's marmalade you give me, I'll give you 50 piastres.'

On hearing the offer, the quarter master decided to play along. He went to the stores and looked for the tins of marmalade. 'There was something funny about the business,' he observed. 'I could only find 14 labels: most of the tins had none. So I gave Killick the labels, and off he went. In about half an hour or so he came back with a wide grin on his face.'

The quarter master was paid 700 piasters but he was still none the wiser. In the following days he noticed that most of the new tins of marmalade arriving in his stores were also missing their labels.

It was two weeks later that he learned the truth. New orders announced that all the men were to have pay deducted to reimburse any of the local people who could produce Tickler's marmalade labels. The Arabs had been led to believe that the marmalade labels were English pound notes and had accepted them in payment for food.[7]

In the Jordan valley Allenby continued to press his men forward following the plan that General Smuts had helped to devise. But progress was slow and 'expensive' in human lives. Had the plan been allowed to continue, the Turkish forces would no doubt have been forced to pull back little by little. They were, after all, heavily outnumbered.

But it was not to be. Changes far away in Europe were to have a sudden and dramatic effect on the campaign.

12

The War Cabinet

Then from the jaws of dragon and beast and false prophet I saw
three foul spirits come; they looked like frogs and in fact were demon
spirits, able to work miracles, going out to all the kings of the world
to call them together for the war of the Great Day of God the
Almighty.

Revelation 16:13–14

Major Tudor Pole had been wounded on 3 December 1917,
just six days before the fall of Jerusalem. It may have been
as he lay recovering in Cairo that he first heard of the
threat to 'Abdu'l-Bahá's life. In what form the news
reached him we do not know. But he must have felt it was
serious. On 24 December he wrote to an influential
acquaintance in England. The letter to Sir Mark Sykes, MP,
would take 43 days to reach its destination.

> On returning to Cairo from the hills round Jerusalem,
> having received the close attentions of a Sniper in a fig
> tree; I ran across my friend Mohi-el-Dine Sabri. He was
> anxious to send you his greeting and friendly remem-
> brances and I promised to oblige. The Turkish Line will
> probably run through Haifa shortly . . . the Bahai leader
> and his family are in imminent danger and at the
> moment, of course, we are powerless. His position and

prestige is not understood among the Authorities here. It is not even realized that he controls a remarkable religious movement, wholly devoid of political and military associations; which can number many millions of adherents throughout the Near and Middle East. Jews, Moslems of various Sects, Christians, Parsis, Hindoos, Kurds unite under the Bahai banner of Spiritual Fellowship. May not these people contribute much, later, to the harmonising of Sectarian and Oriental Religious feuds? Is it too much to ask the Authorities at home to request the Authorities here to afford Abdul Baha every protection and consideration? Anxious enquiries reach me from America, England, France, Russia, Persia, India. A word from Whitehall works wonders. I am your obedient servant, W. Tudor-Pole 2/Lt. 16th Royal Devons. (In hospital).[1]

On recovering sufficiently, Tudor Pole joined the Intelligence Service in Cairo. There he processed and correlated information about the situation behind Turkish lines. This information included reports from spotter planes, the statements of captured soldiers, official papers and intercepted radio communications.[2] Only when this information was brought together could it supply a reliable picture of what was going on.

The defeats of the Turkish army at Gaza, Beersheba, Jaffa and Jerusalem had sapped Djemal Pasha's authority. Enver Pasha and Talaat Pasha were moving against him, undermining his position. At last, early in 1918, Djemal Pasha left Palestine. But the threat to 'Abdu'l-Bahá only seemed to increase.

'. . . news reaching me concerning 'Abdu'l-Bahá's imminent danger became more and more alarming,' Tudor Pole reported. 'I tried to arouse interest in the matter among those who were responsible for Intelligence Service activi-

ties . . . I also brought the matter before my own chief,
General Sir Arthur Money . . .'[3]

But Tudor Pole's superior officers were not interested.
They had a new problem to worry about. Russia had
pulled out of the war, freeing up German troops to serve
on the western front. The British War Cabinet became
alarmed and abruptly pulled most of Allenby's best troops
back to Europe. The plan devised by Smuts and Allenby
was over.

Allenby's army looked as if it was going nowhere. The
seasoned fighters were gone. The men who had been sent
to take their place were inexperienced and ill equipped.

Many observers of the time would have taken one look
at the new men and given up hope. Though experience
might be acquired with time and supplies could be pro-
cured, nothing could be done about their race – for the
new troops were mostly dark skinned.

At that time, Allenby's new soldiers would have had a
hard time serving in the British army. When dark-skinned
recruits arrived on the western front they were usually
treated as inferior. It was not just a matter of race. Religious prejudices also came into play. Many of these men
were Hindus, Sikhs and Muslims from India.

Allenby now had troops from many different countries
and territories: Britain, Australia, New Zealand, India,
Hong Kong, Singapore, France, Italy, South Africa, the
West Indies and Egypt. There was even a detachment of
Rarotongan islanders from the Pacific who manned the
surf boats which brought in supplies to the harbourless sections of the coast.[4] Allied against him was an army of
Turks, Germans, Austrians and Arabs. Palestine had
become a microcosm of what history would rightly call the

First World War.

One of Allenby's greatest victories, therefore, was that he managed to have the new men rapidly and successfully integrated into the existing regiments. Language and cultural barriers were overcome and mutual respect and trust – vital for men fighting alongside each other in battle – were quickly established.

Allenby continued to probe the Turkish defences, sending a mixture of new and experienced troops out on sorties. Not only did this stop his enemy relaxing, it brought in first class intelligence and built up the experience of the new men under real fire.

The response to Tudor Pole's first letter was slow in coming. In the meantime he found another method of getting a message back to England. At a sports club in Alexandria he ran into a Foreign Office official, Major David Ormsby Gore, who was willing to help. Major Gore was soon to return to England and agreed to carry a letter by hand.

This was a risky move for both men. Smuggling an uncensored letter out of Egypt could lead to a court martial. And for Tudor Pole the charge would look particularly serious. He was attempting to bypass the chain of command by going over the heads of his superior officers.

The letter was carried first to Lady Paget, who sent it on to her son-in-law, Lord Plymouth, who in turn took it directly to Lord Balfour, a member of the War Cabinet. Balfour arranged to have it put on the agenda of a meeting in which he, the prime minister and Lord Curzon were present.[5]

At the same time, the Bahá'í community in Britain,

having been alerted to the danger, began to lobby on 'Abdu'l-Bahá's behalf. One prominent Bahá'í, Lady Blomfield, contacted Lord Lamington, who in turn wrote to Lord Balfour.

> I have been asked to intervene in the interest of Abdul Behar.
> I enclose a Memo. about him and I should be grateful could the action indicated be taken.

The memorandum read:

> Abdul Behar sometimes known as Abbas Effendi, leader of the Bahai movement, having for its object the true peace of the world, is believed to be at his home in Haifa, or else on M. Carmel. In the past he has undergone much persecution at the hands of fanatics and anxiety is felt by his many friends in Gt. Britain and America lest he, his wife and family should not receive adequate protection during the British advance owing to his identity not being known to our authorities. His friends therefore would be grateful if instructions would be cabled to secure on his behalf the good offices of those in command.[6]

'Abdu'l-Bahá had won many influential admirers in Britain before the war. These people were now given a chance to act on behalf of the Bahá'í leader. Mrs Whyte, who had invited 'Abdu'l-Bahá to Edinburgh in 1913, learned of the news and promptly got in touch with her son, Frederick Whyte, a member of parliament. Her son then contacted the Foreign Office.

> I have just received a letter from my Mother saying that she understands that Abdul Baha is living in some risk of his life at Haifa. My Mother's correspondent, as you will see from the enclosed letter, seems to think that we could

do something to save him. I presume I need not waste your time in giving an account of Abdul Baha himself, whose personality and work must be well known to you. But as you are aware, he has a good many followers, if one may so call them, in this country; and in general there is a number of people who, like myself, are much interested in his work and will be prepared to do something to make sure that the Military Authorities in Palestine are aware of his presence. I know that at one time Lord Curzon was very deeply impressed with the Bahai Movement in Persia itself and he may be willing to interest himself in the matter now.[7]

Thus by at least three routes Tudor Pole managed to get the news of 'Abdu'l-Bahá's situation through to the British government. These communications, arriving around the same time as each other, had the desired effect and a message was promptly telegraphed back to Egypt, telling the military authorities of 'Abdu'l-Bahá's presence and instructing them that 'he and his family should be treated with special consideration in the event of our occupying Haiffa'.[8]

On its journey the message passed through Tudor Pole's own hands before reaching its destination. But, as he wryly observed, 'No one at Headquarters had heard of 'Abdu'l-Bahá or of the Bahá'í Movement.'[9]

The message was then passed back to the Intelligence Service with a request for background information. Tudor Pole was the only person who knew anything about the subject so he was given the task of providing General Allenby with the relevant information. This he was glad to do.

But there was little that the British authorities could do except to make it known behind enemy lines that stern retribution would follow any attempt to cause death or injury to 'Abdu'l-Bahá.[10]

So long as the Turkish authorities controlled the Haifa area, 'Abdu'l-Bahá would remain in serious danger. And if the British succeeded in advancing towards Haifa the death sentence might well be triggered. The only hope seemed to be a very rapid and completely unexpected British advance – an event sudden enough to give the Turkish authorities no chance to carry out Djemal Pasha's threat.

Of all the advances during the First World War, none had been as rapid as the one needed to save the life of 'Abdu'l-Bahá.

13

Inspiration

They called the kings together at the place, called in Hebrew, Armageddon.

Revelation 16:16

On 1 August 1918 Allenby returned from his morning ride and called the senior officers together. He had worked out a new plan in his head. This time they would not try to capture a few miles of land or a handful of towns and villages. This time he wanted to finish the whole campaign in one go.

The Turkish forces were organized in three parts, the 8th Army near the coast, the 7th Army in the Judæan hills and the 4th Army in the Jordan valley. Allenby's objective would be to wipe out all three, together with supporting German and Austrian units.

Allenby was a religious man who knew the Bible well. The significance of the proposed battle plan did not escape him. For if things were to go as he hoped, the trap would close in the mountainous area around the town of Megiddo – the place 'called in Hebrew, Armageddon'.

Not only that – the armies he was fighting had come south from the area of the ancient city of Babylon, crossing the Euphrates River, just as was mentioned in chapter 16 of the book of Revelation.

Nor can he have failed to see the similarity between the vision in Revelation and the appearance of modern warfare. How else could St John have described an artillery barrage but as being like thunder, lightning, violent earthquakes and massive hailstones falling from the sky?

From his letters, it is clear that Allenby was well-informed about biblical prophecy. 'Several people wrote to me', he recalled, 'before I took Jerusalem, in 1917; to say that it was the 1335th year and that Daniel's prophecy would come true.'[1]

Then in another letter: 'I am interested in what you say about the Second Coming as being near. The "Signs of the Times" are certainly such as are mentioned in connection with it.'[2]

'Abdu'l-Bahá had also commented on the prophecies in detail, identifying some as literal and others as symbolic. For example, the Battle of Armageddon was the literal fighting of the First World War.[3] The New Jerusalem, however, was not a physical structure ready to descend from the sky.

'This is what is meant in the Bible by the descent of the New Jerusalem,' 'Abdu'l-Bahá explained.

> The heavenly Jerusalem is none other than divine civilization, and it is now ready. It is to be and shall be organized, and the oneness of humankind will be a visible fact. Humanity will then be brought together as one. The various religions will be united, and different races will be known as one kind. The Orient and the Occident will be conjoined, and the banner of international peace will be unfurled. The world shall at last find peace, and the

equalities and rights of men shall be established.[4]

Allenby's new plan was a complete reversal of all the troops had been doing before. Instead of pushing on across the Jordan valley, they would punch north along the coastal plain where the mobility of the cavalry could be used to best advantage. If they could travel with great speed, it might be possible to cut off their enemy's lines of retreat at the Musmus Pass and Jenin.

To achieve the speed of breakthrough which he needed, Allenby wanted four times the strength of his opponent over the length of the five mile front where the attack was to take place. If the Turks realized what he was doing, they could simply reinforce their own lines and Allenby's task would be impossible.

Yet again, the whole idea would succeed or fail on the question of secrecy. Under the Smuts/Allenby plan, the attack was to take place in the Jordan valley far to the east. Under the new plan, the attack would come far to the west. Allenby had the problem of moving large numbers of troops across Palestine without the Turks or Germans detecting them. Having been deceived by Allenby at Beersheba, they were not going to be taken in so easily again. Spies were thought to be operating regularly, some coming through the front line and others walking through the desert to pass round the open eastern flank.[5]

Perhaps these spies saw the engineering operations near Jaffa. Many bridges were built over rivers in the area then taken down, built once more and taken down again. It must have seemed as if the men were being trained in preparation for the crossing of the Jordan. What spies could not have seen was that two of the bridges were of more solid construction than the rest. These two were not dismantled.

Another risk to Allenby's plan was the activities of enemy spotter planes. One man walking would throw up a small cloud of dust. A troop of marching men could make a cloud visible from miles away. It was the job of 'policemen' to watch for aeroplanes. On the sound of a distant engine they would blow whistles and everyone would stop moving to let the dust die down. If the plane proved to be friendly, the 'policemen' would blow again for the all clear.

Lawrence of Arabia did his bit to make the deception more convincing. He sent thousands of gold sovereigns to the Arabs on the east side of the Jordan valley, asking to purchase all the barley on their threshing floors. He recalled 'begging them not to mention it, but we would require it for our animals and for our British allies, in a fortnight'. News of that kind spreads fast, as it was intended to. 'Dhiab of Tafileh – that jerky, incomplete hobbledehoy – gossiped the news instantly . . .'[6]

And so the trickery went on. No one will ever know how many of the small details were picked up by German or Turkish intelligence. Did they discover, as they were meant to, that a hotel in Jerusalem had been vacated as if being made ready to act as GHQ, complete with rooms allocated and telephones installed and connected? Did they notice columns of West Indian soldiers daily leaving Jerusalem on a long march down into the Jordan valley? Certainly they knew nothing of the lorry rides these same soldiers took each night, back to their starting position.

Did they perhaps observe 15,000 horses on the eastern flank of Allenby's army, or see the dust as these beasts were supposedly led to water every day? Had they looked closer they might have seen that these 'horses' were no more than stick frameworks covered in blankets, the dust clouds made by mules dragging wooden sledges.

Great tent camps were erected which housed no more than a handful of men whose task it was to move about conspicuously during the day and tend all the camp fires at night.

Near Jaffa the deception was exactly the other way about. Men were hidden – crammed into a small number of tents and only permitted to use smokeless fuel for their camp fires.

In the days before the attack, Lawrence rode with his Arab fighters to blow up sections of the Hejaz railway behind Turkish lines. The deception seemed to be working because enemy troops started moving from Haifa to reinforce positions in the Jordan valley.

The men themselves knew nothing of Allenby's plans but all understood that the enemy was being deceived. For them it was a great game. But dangerous also, as the lives of tens of thousands hung in the balance. One whisper would have been enough to make the enemy suspicious. Then, with a few further checks, the whole deception would have been revealed.

Allenby enforced secrecy with all the considerable force of his personality. Anything could be a risk – a wandering Arab allowed into a restricted area or an injudicious comment in a letter home. Even if indiscretions were not picked up by the enemy, the British authorities would court martial the careless soldier.

At last the time came for Allenby to reveal the true extent of the plan to his senior officers. One of them remembered seeing 'the expression of astonishment on the

faces of the Cavalry Brigade and Regimental Commanders when they heard, two days before the operation, the
scope of the role allotted to them'.[7]

Then, one day before the attack was to take place, the
rest of the men were informed. For one sergeant in particular the news was a shock. As a deeply committed Muslim,
he felt it his religious duty to inform his co-religionists of
what was about to happen. On the eve of the battle, he
slipped away from his unit, crossed the front line and told
the Turks everything he knew.

The Turkish commanders believed him. Now all they
had to do was withdraw the bulk of their troops from the
front lines back to a secondary line of defence. When the
attack came, the British guns would waste their fire battering
empty trenches and the British troops would unknowingly
advance towards fresh positions.[8]

14

Armageddon

So the angel set his sickle to work on the earth and harvested the whole vintage of the earth and put it into a huge winepress, the winepress of God's anger, outside the city, where it was trodden until the blood that came out of the winepress was up to the horses' bridles as far away as two hundred miles.

Revelation 14:19–20

Lieutenant Wilson lay on the beach in front of his horse, waiting for the dawn. The unit had moved into position under the cover of night. Though still well back from the front, every man was keyed up for the attack.

At that moment, in the silence that precedes the storm, he could look back on three of the most agreeable days of the entire campaign. They had been camped amid the orange groves, in the pleasant shade of trees heavy with delicious fruit. All that had been required of them was to stay out of sight of enemy aircraft, groom their horses, clean their weapons – and rest.[1]

Wilson could hear the contented champing of horses on bits and could just see in the brilliant moonlight some of the nine thousand horsemen whose closely formed lines stretched back for about three miles along the beach.[2]

His own unit, the 13th Cavalry Brigade, had a particular assignment. His were new orders, changed only the day before. The knowledge of his special role kept him at a high pitch of excitement – in spite of having what he described as 'the father and mother of all headaches'. A tourniquet tied around the forehead served to make the pain liveable.

Even for soldiers used to General Allenby's style, the orders must have seemed extraordinary. Instead of a barrage lasting several days, the bombardment would take only minutes. It would be short but intense, involving 385 artillery pieces on land and the guns of two Royal Navy destroyers in the Mediterranean. Then the infantry would start their advance.

The cavalry would charge forward as soon as a hole had been punched in the Turkish defences. Timing was critical. Charge too soon and they would get caught up with the infantry. Too late and the gap might have closed again. It was known as 'hitting the G in the Gap'.

When the cavalry were through, some would help the infantry to consolidate their victory by outflanking and rolling up the line on each side of the breakthrough. All the rest were to ride north, deep into enemy territory. On finding pockets of resistance, they were to go around them. Speed was everything.

At 3:55 a.m. on 19 September the moon set and the men emerged silently from their tents and shelters. Gaps had already been cut in the British wire. Each was marked with tape so the infantry could find them in the dark and line up in the correct places.

A Handley-Page bomber flew north over the lines. This was a new kind of plane, capable of carrying 1200 lbs of bombs.[3] Its targets were lines of communication, including the main telephone exchange. By this it was hoped that news of the attack could be delayed.

The sky above the Judæan hills began to show the pink flush of dawn. It was a few seconds short of 4:30 a.m. Allenby looked at his watch. Five, four, three, two, one. The general's voice boomed out 'Zero' and all the guns began to fire. Within minutes further aeroplanes were roaring overhead on their way north.

At 4:45 the infantry started to advance, cutting the Turkish barbed wire by hand where it had not been flattened by the shell fire. Their advance was so rapid and unexpected that some of the Turkish guns never fired, while those that did hit ground through which the attacking infantry had already passed.

Lieutenant Wilson and the rest of the Royal Gloucester Hussars (part of the 13th Cavalry Regiment) had expected to move forward late in the morning but the order to mount and gallop came at 5:30 a.m. Within an hour they were passing through the enemy entrenchments. Each carried a limited amount of food for man and beast; once that was used they would have to take what they needed from the local population.

Some of the cavalry which followed them swung to the left and right to widen the gap in the Turkish defences and outflank the front line. Others fought their way through to a second line of defence in the marshes, then on north towards the Musmus pass, 35 miles away.

Wilson's regiment, along with two others, had a different objective. They travelled light – all their field guns and supply trucks had been left to follow later. In the spearhead of the cavalry, they worked their way past the second line of defence by riding along the beach. Then on north, fast and secretly.

For the German High Command in Nazareth, the events of the previous month had painted a clear picture. The British army was moving troops towards the Jordan valley. The expected attack would undoubtedly be another eastward push – an attempt to cut the Hejaz railway. When and if an attack came near the coast it would be easy to fall back to Mount Carmel. Even a small force would be able to defend the Musmus pass. The British would be held up there for months. A large garrison in Haifa was available as a reserve force if needed. Von Sanders, the Commander-in-Chief of German-Turkish forces, must have felt quietly confident.

Then, on 18 September, news came through that an Indian sergeant had deserted from the British army and was warning of an imminent British attack near the coast. Several of the senior Turkish commanders believed the story to be true and were begging von Sanders to allow them to withdraw their troops to a second line of defence.

But the German Commander-in-Chief was not about to give up miles of land without a fight – especially when he considered the sergeant's story to be another of Allenby's clever tricks.[4]

Soon after dawn on 19 September von Sanders began to receive reports of an attack near the coast. Then the telephone lines went dead. He still did not realize what was happening but, as a precaution, he sent a column of over five hundred infantry to march up and install machine guns in the Musmus Pass. He also ordered that a watch be kept on the roads leading into Nazareth. He was to receive no further news of the battle until the following morning.

By the afternoon of the 19th, Wilson and his men had reached a small village where they could rest until evening, unobserved by Turkish aeroplanes. They consulted local Jews and Arabs and eventually managed to buy the services of two Arab guides who promised to lead them by a concealed route across Mount Carmel.

With evening approaching they moved on. Goat tracks were the only means of crossing the steep and rocky mountain. Some of the passes proved to be so narrow that pack horses had to be unloaded before they could squeeze through. As night fell, each man had to struggle to keep the horse in front in view. When at 2:15 a.m. the brigadier called a halt, he found that only a handful of men were present. Guides were sent back and eventually two of the three missing regiments were found.

While Wilson and his men had been galloping north along the beach, other cavalry units were pushing forward further inland. There was only sporadic resistance and they moved fast. Their objective, the Musmus Pass, was the key to the whole plan. If they could reach it quickly, they hoped to be able to attack the Turkish defences before they were reinforced.

By 10:00 p.m. on the first day, advanced patrols had already reached the slope of the Mount Carmel ridge. Amid the confusion of the rapid advance and hampered by the dark, some units overshot the entrance to the Musmus Pass and had to be fetched back. It was thus a much smaller force that rode on into the pass, lighted on its way by the moon. The moon slipped lower towards the horizon as they picked their way forward. At last the road was swallowed by deep black shadow and they were left with only the starlight to help them. The dark would hide both the advancing cavalry and any Turkish troops defending the pass. It was the sound of the horses' hooves that was most likely to give warning of the attack.

Steeled ready for the fight, with all senses straining to detect the position of their enemy, the cavalry rode on through the pass. It was a journey of several miles to the town of Megiddo on the other side of the Carmel ridge. Amazingly, as they emerged at Megiddo there was still no opposition. The place was deserted.

The Turkish infantry arrived the following morning. The sun rose to reveal a column of over five hundred men advancing across the plain. In the narrow confines of the mountains the infantry would have held out easily, but on open ground, they had no chance. The cavalry charged out across the flat land, through patches of cultivation, leaping over small streams. The Turkish battalion was cut to pieces. Forty-six men were lanced to death and the remaining 470 surrendered with all their weapons.[5]

In the early hours of the morning, with the moon setting, Lieutenant Wilson and his men descended the north side of Mount Carmel and arrived within sight of their goal – Nazareth, the German headquarters. It had been an exhausting and tortuous route but they were still unobserved, having avoided von Sanders's waiting guards.

They crossed the plain through a series of small villages. At each one they were forced to leave men behind to guard prisoners and make sure no warning could be telephoned through to Nazareth. They were a tired and very much reduced force, without heavy guns and at the very end of their supplies.

They arrived at their goal just under 24 hours after the attack had begun. With swords drawn, they charged down the streets of Nazareth hoping to capture the German Commander-in-Chief.

The plan for this daring raid had been made so late that no maps had been provided. The hunt for Liman von Sanders would have to be haphazard.

Wilson and his men searched through an army barracks. Their arrival was so unexpected that the occupants had no chance to arm themselves. One hundred and fifty Turkish soldiers were rounded up straight away. One of the prisoners pointed to an upper storey of the building. Wilson left a trooper to guard the stairs and proceeded alone to a long corridor with about 20 rooms on each side.

The band was still around Wilson's head, his clothes were dusty and his chin covered in bristly stubble. Gripping a revolver in each hand, he advanced, feeling more like a pirate than a cavalry officer.

On throwing open the first door, he was met by an officer who bowed politely before handing over a revolver and a sword. Wilson sent him down to the trooper waiting at the foot of the stairs. He then threw open the second door and found another officer who dutifully surrendered. By the time he reached the last door there were several heaps of weapons in the corridor.

The last room, however, was different. The door was locked and he heard the murmur of voices from inside. He felt sure the room could not be taken easily. Steeling himself for the fight, he threw his full weight against the door and burst into the room.

There he saw a man on his knees, hands clasped in prayer. A naked woman lay on the bed with a newborn

baby beside her. Wilson was utterly defeated. All he could
do was shake hands with the man, pat the woman on the
head and leave them to themselves. Before he departed he
pinned a note to the door warning all troopers to leave the
family in peace.

Not far distant, two excited nuns were addressing a
British officer in voluble French. They kept pointing to an
upstairs room but could not make the Englishman understand. 'All right,' the officer soothed. 'Presently. Presently.'[6]

The officer soon escaped the clutches of the two nuns
and headed off on more important work. As soon as he
was out of sight, Liman von Sanders, still wearing pyjamas,
slipped out of the building and away to organize his men.[7]

It did not take the German Commander-in-Chief long
to discover that the British had failed to get through the
town to cut off his escape.[8]

The British searched for von Sanders in vain and at last
gave up. Resistance was beginning to stiffen so they with-
drew from Nazareth with some two thousand prisoners to
wait for reinforcements. They did later realize their mistake
but wisely decided not to tell Allenby how the German
Commander-in-Chief had escaped. Instead they reported
that he had left town before they arrived.

During the second day after the attack, the Australian
Mounted Division came through the Musmus Pass and
turned east, some of them passing through El'Affule,
barely seven miles south of Nazareth.

When Wilson entered this town, he reported seeing evidence of their passing:

Unfortunately the Australians had been there before us

and, having a natural 'nose' for gold, had swiped all they could carry of the beautiful golden sovereigns. The place was littered with paper money but we realized with the departure of the Turks this currency was now worthless.[9]

On emerging from the Musmus pass, another group of Australians headed for the strategic town of Jenin, the only remaining escape route for the retreating forces west of the Jordan. Once in Jenin, they only had to sit and wait for the Turkish army to come to them.

During the evening of the second day, while the Australians were digging in at Jenin, a group of 23 men got lost in the poor light. They were horrified to see advancing towards them in the moonlight, 2800 retreating Germans and Turks. Withdrawing looked dangerous so they decided to bluff it out. They first fired a burst of machine gun bullets into the air, then called on the advancing column to surrender. The dispirited troops, having marched many miles along rocky mountain tracks, now found their way blocked by a force of unknown strength. They were trapped in a narrow ravine with sides too steep to climb.

With a German nurse acting as interpreter, the Australians stated that they were at the front of an overwhelming force who were out of sight in the shadows. The Germans and Turks surrendered, concluding that their enemies must have been landed at Haifa by the 'wonderful British Navy'. They could not imagine a force reaching Jenin so quickly any other way.

15

The Most Terrible Plague

Every island vanished and the mountains disappeared; and hail, with great hailstones weighing a talent[1] each, fell from the sky on people. They cursed God for sending a plague of hail; it was the most terrible plague.

Revelation 16:21

By the evening of the second day the Turkish 7th and 8th Armies were almost cut off. To escape north they would have to cross the mountains around Megiddo. But the Musmus pass and Jenin were already held by the British and Australian cavalry.

Only one way remained open: the narrow tracks winding eastward through the mountains towards the Jordan valley. Soon most of the Turkish 7th Army were moving along these in a great column many miles long, followed closely by the advancing British.

The Turkish 7th Army met its end in the narrow confines of a steep sided wadi. Every available British plane took part in the slaughter, bombing first the front of the column and blocking the road, then returning to systematically destroy trapped machines, animals and men.

Two bombers flew over the wadi every two minutes dropping 20 lb and 112 lb bombs,[2] with additional flights of six machines each half hour. From four o'clock in the morning until nearly midday there was a continuous succession of explosions along with fire from the planes' machine guns.

'I dived and fired continually on the thickest part of the column,' reported one airman. 'They were literally sprayed and I succeeded in inflicting heavy casualties.'

Another bomber pilot recalled his part in the slaughter: 'Four direct hits, one in a body of cavalry roughly 50 strong; the bomb appeared to have practically demolished them as less than 6 got up and ran away.'[3]

Some of the pilots were so appalled by what they were doing that they asked to be released from duty.

A reporter saw the wadi on the following day. 'It was horrible,' he recalled.

> Thousands of dead animals already made the air offensive. Horses, oxen, mules, and donkeys had met sudden deaths as they stood anchored in that long-drawn-out column of transport. There were signs of panic, for some beasts had swung out of the line and had hurled themselves with their loads over the precipice into the bed of the wadi, while other frightened creatures had made a desperate effort to haul the vehicles attached to them up the rocky hills. There was scarcely anything standing on wheels except guns, and not all of these had survived the bombs.[4]

The scene called to mind the prophecies of the Bible, particularly the vision of Isaiah:

> For the indignation of the Lord is upon all nations, and his fury upon all their armies; he hath utterly destroyed them, he hath delivered them to the slaughter. Their slain also shall be cast out, and their stink shall come up out of

their carcasses, and the mountains shall be melted with their blood.[5]

Similar scenes were enacted along other escape routes, so that within 72 hours of the initial attack, two out of the three Turkish armies had been completely wiped out.

The Turkish 4th Army, which held the east bank of the Jordan, remained intact. It was also thought that there were strong garrisons in Acre and the port of Haifa. Allenby's army was in danger of overextending itself. The men had eaten all the food they had carried. They were surviving by taking what food they could find from the local people. Most of the ammunition had also been used.

With the need to re-supply the army from the sea, Allenby would now turn his mind to Haifa. And now, also, would be the time of greatest danger to 'Abdu'l-Bahá. If Djemal Pasha's order were to be carried out, it would be in the next few days.

The Battle for Haifa

O Lord! Have pity on these ignorant ones and look upon them with the eye of forgiveness and pardon. Extinguish this fire, so that these dense clouds which obscure the horizon may be scattered, the Sun of Reality shine forth with the rays of conciliation, this intense gloom be dispelled and the resplendent light of peace shed its radiance upon all countries.

'Abdu'l-Bahá[1]

The people of Haifa had received no real news in months. The official line stated that the Turkish army was about to push south and take the Suez Canal. Few people believed it.

Then there were the British propaganda leaflets, dropped from aeroplanes. They claimed that the German people were not descended from the Prophet Muḥammad after all. They also stated that the British were achieving great victories and would surely win the war.

The only thing that the people could be sure of was what they saw with their own eyes. The principal Turkish and German reserves were stationed in the town. Guns had been set up in strategic positions. German military engineers were installing a battery of big naval guns on top of Mount Carmel, ready to sink any warships that tried to take Haifa from the sea. Even if Britain's propaganda were correct and its army did arrive, it would not take Haifa easily. True, the Turkish troops were badly clothed and hungry but that was just the same as everyone else in Palestine.

Then, on the afternoon of 21 September, the atmosphere suddenly changed. Soldiers gathered, quickly, urgently. They assembled late in the day and started marching out of town along the Nazareth road.

What the people could not have known was that Nazareth had been attacked. The German headquarters had promptly sent a message to Haifa calling for reinforcements. After the message came through, the radio went dead. Telephone lines were also out of action. The reinforcements left Haifa in the evening, marched 25 miles in the dark and arrived at Nazareth before dawn.

For Allenby, the battle of Armageddon seemed to be going better than he could have hoped. They were three days into the attack and already his men had pushed over 50 miles into Turkish territory. Nothing of the kind had happened during the war – for any army on any front.

But success brought new problems. His cavalry had taken with them only enough food for three days. Now, with the food almost exhausted and ammunition low, they had advanced far out of reach of their supply dumps. Food was being carted up from the south but the roads were poor and the gradients steep. The supplies could not keep up. If the port of Haifa could not be taken quickly, supplies could not be landed from the sea and the advance would need to be reined in.

Allenby's efforts to disrupt communications had also been hugely successful. He now advanced into territory without working telephone lines and his own troops suffered the consequences. His engineers worked in small, fast-moving groups to repair the lines, sometimes just behind the cavalry, sometimes level with them – and occasionally, by mistake, in front of them.

Then, around dawn on 22 September, Turkish and German troops launched a counter-attack on Nazareth. The fighting was intense and bloody but Allenby's men were well dug in by that time and managed to drive the enemy off, killing or capturing many.

The Turkish and German troops said that they had marched from the garrison in Haifa. Around the same time, news started to filter through from the local population that Haifa and Acre had been abandoned.[2]

It was what the British had hoped for. Brigadier-General King set out in his armoured Rolls Royce to take control of the town. He was accompanied by only a light armoured motor battery and a light car patrol.

As they approached Haifa they discovered a group of 69 Turkish soldiers busy laying explosives on one of the bridges. The Turks surrendered without a fight. The brigadier must still have believed he was going to drive into the town and claim the victory. It was not to be. With only a few miles to go, the brigadier and his men came under a fierce and sustained attack. They only just managed to escape but had to abandon several damaged vehicles – including the Rolls Royce.

When the people of Haifa heard the gunfire they knew the end was near. The British were coming and it seemed most likely that the town would be razed to the ground. Now was also the time when Djemal Pasha's death sentence on 'Abdu'l-Bahá might be carried out. The town was still full

of Turks, including many spies.[3] Anyone who carried out
the death sentence might win favour with Djemal Pasha,
still one of the three most powerful men in the Ottoman
Empire. The small and terrified Bahá'í community gathered in the house of 'Abdu'l-Bahá.

It was a simple building, with the rooms built off a large
central hall. The hall was pleasantly cool, even in summer.
A large arched window looked out onto a small garden
courtyard. The decoration too was simple, almost sparse.
The entire house had only one real carpet and that lay, for
the benefit of guests, on the floor of the reception room.

'Abdu'l-Bahá calmed the excited Bahá'ís and called
them to prayer. Then He assured them that all would be
well and that no British shells would cause death or
damage to the population of Haifa. At an earlier meeting
He had even predicted that the strongly fortified city of
Acre would be taken by the British almost without blood-
shed – by two unarmed soldiers.[4]

The story goes that two soldiers who had become separ-
ated from their companions did indeed arrive in Acre,
believing it to be in British hands. Perhaps they were army
engineers repairing damaged telephone lines. As with
Jerusalem, the mayor was anxious to rid himself of the
responsibility for law and order in the town and tried to
surrender the keys of the city to the hapless men. But they,
not understanding the language, dropped the keys and fled
in panic.[5]

On 23 September a larger British force arrived in the area.
It split into two, the larger part advancing on Haifa. The
smaller part, including Lieutenant Wilson, headed for
Acre. Wilson had now survived five exhausting days on

three days' rations and little sleep. As he and his men approached Acre they reached a settlement where they were delayed.

'The war was held up for an hour or so', he recalled, 'when we were entertained by some very pretty dancing ladies at a small village where we had found some water for our horses. The dancers and musicians were really very good, the instruments tuneful and the little episode served as a tonic.' But he had few illusions as to the motive of the villagers. 'No doubt, while we were being entertained, someone from the village was running to Haifa and Acre to warn them.'

Wilson could hear a good deal of gunfire from the direction of Haifa but his men met only feeble artillery fire as they approached Acre across the fertile plain. When they arrived they found the Turkish forces had gone and local Arabs were running riot, looting the town. Wilson decided that the only way to restore order would be to shoot some of the troublemakers. Not having the resources to do this, he decided instead to join in the free-for-all.

In the grounds of one factory he found a large tank of olive oil. The crowd of looters was so thick and frantic that one person had been pushed into the tank. 'I could see him blowing bubbles from at least three feet below the surface.' This did not stop Wilson taking a bucketful of oil for himself, which he then exchanged for an egg with an old lady. The lady was too frail to take part in the push and shove around the oil tank. Wilson went back to the tank several times and was able to barter the oil for a good supply of eggs, some fruit and even a chicken, all of which he took back to his regiment.[6]

The remaining officials gladly handed the town over to

the British and order was gradually restored. For the thirteenth time in its long history, Acre had fallen. This time hardly a shot had been fired.

Haifa would not be taken so easily. It was defended by fresh troops led by officers who understood the strategic significance of the port. Haifa was also a natural fortress, protected on three sides by the steep mountain slope, the sea and stretches of treacherous marshland. The only way between the marshes and Mount Carmel was a narrow and vulnerable corridor, easily defended.

The attacking cavalry advanced down this corridor until they came under fire from machine guns and artillery, including that installed on the crest of the mountain. To go further down that road would have been suicide so they split into four groups. The first made a wide sweep to the north aiming to outflank the guns and ride into the town via the beach, the second tried to find a way through the marshes and the third attempted to climb the mountain and attack the big gun battery. The remainder waited for the charge into Haifa. With the cavalry was a battery of light artillery which occupied itself by firing on any targets which presented themselves.

The people of Haifa could hear the rumble of heavy guns firing from the summit of Mount Carmel. They could also see shells from the British light artillery falling into the sea, as the gunners fired at Turkish emplacements hidden among the palm groves on the shore. Mistakenly putting the two together, the Haifa residents believed the British were shelling the town from over the mountain. They were terrified, expecting Haifa to be devastated.

In fact, no damage was done as the shelling was never aimed at the town. It was Allenby's policy not to alienate the local population, which was in general glad to be rid of Turkish rule.

The cavalry who tried to follow goat tracks up the mountain did not have an easy time. It was good terrain for goats but not for horses, a great number of which did not make it to the top. Even the men found some of the paths easier to follow on hands and knees. The climb took almost three hours.

Once at the top, some of the men had to dismount to operate the machine guns. Thus out of two squadrons of cavalry which started the climb, only 15 men remained to charge towards the gun batteries.

For the cavalry advancing parallel to the road through the marshes, things were no easier. Their scouts had retreated under heavy machine gun fire, so when the rest of the unit trotted forward, it was without any knowledge of the terrain they were about to experience. By the time they had drawn level with the machine guns (established at the foot of the mountain, on the other side of the road), they were getting bogged down in the marshes. Two of the horses and their riders became stuck, sank and then drowned in the marsh.

The commander, finding himself in a disastrous situation, made a snap decision to wheel round to the left and charge across the road towards the machine guns. It should have been suicide but coming suddenly and being completely unexpected, most of the defending infantry scattered in fright and all the machine gunners were killed.

At about the same time the 15 cavalrymen who had made it to the top of the mountain were charging the big guns. They too succeeded.

With the Turkish and German defences much reduced, the main body of British cavalry was free to ride into Haifa.

Being charged down by men on horses must have been a terrifying experience. The greater the number of riders, the more frightening it would have been. The number of cavalry left for the final attack was so much reduced that some of the engineers were invited to take up lances and ride along with them. These men had no training in the use of the lance. They were not expected to inflict any actual damage but simply to make the body of men more intimidating.

The cavalry thought of themselves as the cream of the forces and no such invitation had ever been made before. The engineers must have felt themselves honoured, for they accepted with enthusiasm.

The cavalry charge led them right into the town, and they were soon joined by the other troops. Galloping through town they attacked anyone who showed signs of resistance. A few were killed but most surrendered, stunned by the speed and ferocity of the attack. One of the mounted engineers did claim later to have killed a Turkish soldier but this was never independently verified.

The looting started almost immediately – worse here than had been seen in other towns. The Bedouin Arabs were particularly active and it took time before they understood the new authorities would not tolerate such behaviour. In the dangerous and chaotic minutes that followed the takeover, cavalry outriders searched through the town for 'Abdu'l-Bahá, fearing that they might be too late.

It was not so. The taking of Haifa had occurred with

such unexpected speed that the orders of Djemal Pasha
had not been carried out. Nor had any of 'Abdu'l-Bahá's
other enemies had a chance to cause any mischief. His
house was eventually located. The Bahá'í leader was found
sitting 'calm and unperturbed' in the forecourt. Other
Bahá'ís were also there, tense and awaiting news. A guard
was immediately set on the house.[7]

Later in the evening the new governor of Jerusalem
came to pay his respects.

News of 'Abdu'l-Bahá's safety was quickly transmitted
to London, informing the government that 'Abdu'l-Bahá
was 'in good health' and 'being well cared for'.[8]

Even though Haifa had been taken, supplies of food
could not be landed immediately. The officer in command
consulted 'Abdu'l-Bahá about the problem.

'I have corn,' said 'Abdu'l-Bahá.

'But for the army?' the astonished officer asked.

'I have corn for the British Army,' 'Abdu'l-Bahá
replied.[9]

With the freedom that came with the change in administration, 'Abdu'l-Bahá was quickly back to work caring for
the poor and needy in Acre and Haifa.

Tudor Pole was soon able to visit 'Abdu'l-Bahá, bringing messages and the gift of a winter cloak. 'He was
looking little older than when I saw him seven years ago,'
Tudor Pole recalled, 'and certainly more vigorous than
when in England after the exhausting American trip.'

His voice is as strong as ever, his step virile, his hair and
beard are (if possible) more silver-white than before . . . I
slept in the room next to 'Abdu'l-Bahá's . . . simple attics
with stone floors and practically no furniture. 'Abdu'l-

Bahá still gives away all money, and lives the life of poverty himself.

. . . I had brought 'Abdu'l-Bahá letters from all parts of the world, and he spent the morning dictating replies for me to take away. I gave him the Persian camel-hair cloak, and it greatly pleased him . . . he had given away the only cloak he possessed. I made him promise to keep this one through the winter anyway, and I trust he does.[10]

17

The Eleventh Hour

Mourn, mourn for this great city; for all the linen and purple and scarlet that you wore, for all your finery of gold and jewels and pearls; your riches are all destroyed within a single hour.

Revelation 18:16

The last remaining opposition to Allenby in Palestine was the Turkish 4th Army. This force, which still held the east side of the Jordan, had only the Hejaz railway on which to escape to Damascus. The line had already been cut in a number of places by Lawrence's Arabs, partly to make the enemy think the attack was coming in the east and partly to hinder the retreat of the 4th Army.

The Judæan hills which had protected the Turks so well from Allenby's army now hemmed them in, removing any threat they might otherwise have posed to the rear of Allenby's army. With the British on one side and desert Arabs attacking from the other, they could not hold out for long.

The Arabs were particularly fierce, taking revenge for the grudges that centuries of Turkish rule had allowed to accumulate. They were nomadic tribes and had no means of holding prisoners. The attacks were prolonged and bloody.

The British cavalry were advancing swiftly towards Damascus with little opposition. There was fighting, some of it fierce, but the German-Turkish army had lost its cohesion and could not put up serious resistance.

Lieutenant Wilson's squadron was again near the forefront of the advance. They had stopped for one night under Mount Hermon where he enjoyed a 'topping bathe in the sea of Galilee'. The water was beautifully fresh, but the bottom was very stony and hard on the feet. He decided that he could not blame anyone for walking on the water there.[1]

The only serious opposition to Allenby's forces came when they reached Damascus. By that time his cavalry were suffering from exhaustion and disease. Malaria and Spanish influenza were rife.

The first attempts to enter the town were fiercely resisted. Then the local population, anticipating an Arab state with Damascus as capital, ran riot. Many of the Turkish soldiers decided it was safer to surrender to Allenby's forces than to hold out against the Arabs.

Damascus fell. The Turkish 4th Army was cut off.

Wilson, riding into Damascus near midnight, found the town lit up like Blackpool. He and his men were soon forced to halt because the crowds were so thick. 'I have never seen such a crowd of naughty girls in my life,' he confessed. 'Cairo, Port Said or Alexandria had nothing on Damascus.'[2]

With plentiful water and greenery, courts and fountains, mosaics and stained glass, Damascus seemed like paradise compared to the surrounding country.[3]

Rejoicing Arabs rode up and down the streets through the night, firing their weapons into the air. Wilson and his men got little sleep.

The call to prayer sounded particularly sweet that night in Damascus. Lawrence, who had taken part in the attack, listened carefully to the words. 'God alone is great: I testify there are no gods but God, and Mohammed is his prophet. Come to prayer, come to security. God alone is great: there is no god but God.' Then the voice became quieter, and added softly: 'And he is very good to us this day, O people of Damascus.'[4]

At first light Wilson and his troops made their escape and continued on the long road towards Aleppo. Shortly afterwards, Wilson developed malaria followed by influenza. He and many other sick and wounded were left in a school building to die. He was without food for some days and had to crawl over a dead body to get water to drink.

Eventually he recovered enough to go out and purchase a meal and his health slowly returned. Writing home soon afterwards, he said: 'Dear Mother, Just a usual report, well and happy, although I have been in dock for three days with a touch of Spanish flu but am glad to say I'm quite all right now.'

After recovering, Lieutenant Wilson returned to England where he married 'Paddie', the VAD nurse whom he had first met in Egypt. It was a long and happy marriage.[5]

The remnants of Allenby's cavalry reached Aleppo, 115 miles further north, on the night of 25 October and, after more fighting, took control.[6] Turkey sued for peace on 31 October. The Ottoman Empire was destroyed.[7]

Eleven days later Germany capitulated and on the eleventh hour of the eleventh day of the eleventh month the First World War was over.

Djemal Pasha fled to Germany. In Turkey, a death sentence was passed against him in his absence. He travelled to Switzerland, then visited Russia and Afghanistan, where he started to rebuild his power base. He was assassinated in July 1922.[8]

After being part of the British delegation at the Paris Peace Conference, Meinertzhagen returned to the Middle East to act as Allenby's political officer.[9]

Wellesley Tudor Pole continued to be interested in the spiritual world and wrote several books on the subject. He never formally accepted the Bahá'í religion, though he often spoke and wrote in support of it. He passed away in 1968 at the age of 84.[10]

'Abdu'l-Bahá remained in Haifa, continuing to give help to all who sought it. Just as advice had previously been offered to members of the Turkish administration, now the British were offered help. Most of their higher echelons came to call on 'Abdu'l-Bahá at one time or another.

Ronald Storrs, Governor of Jerusalem, had the daunting task of finding reliable people to fill posts in the new administration. He turned for advice to 'Abdu'l-Bahá, whom he had met before the war.[11] 'Abdu'l-Bahá recommended to Storrs several of the Bahá'ís for 'positions of confidence', posts where the trust placed in them was then shown to be fully justified.

A life of training in warfare had not prepared General Allenby for the task of civil administration. His jurisdiction was a huge area, full of peoples with conflicting interests and demands, many with unrealistic hopes now the Ottoman Empire had fallen.

Within the districts of his administration one of the most intractable problems was that of the Jews and the Arabs. Britain had made contradictory promises to each side in order to gain their support, something 'Abdu'l-Bahá had specifically advised against:

> The world of humanity owes to the Jews a homestead of their own. Let those who are responsible for kindling the flame in this new hearth see to it that the heat warms and does not scorch both friends and neighbours alike.[12]

But neither side could be placated. Supporters of the Arab cause accused Allenby of favouring the Jews; Jewish supporters believed he was favouring the Arabs.

For a time Allenby took up residence in Haifa and visited 'Abdu'l-Bahá, having long discussions with Him. We will never know what went on between them but some of Allenby's later speeches bore a striking resemblance to the teachings of the Bahá'í religion. Even his phrases and choice of words had become an echo of what he must have heard from 'Abdu'l-Bahá.

'Nationalism', said Allenby, 'is commonly held up to admiration; praised as a high – perhaps the highest – virtue; while internationalism is often branded as a crime, a surrender, a betrayal of our own peculiar interests and rights . . .'

> Nations now maintain internal peace and good order by means of their own organized police forces . . . To an unprejudiced and dispassionate observer there can be, however, no obvious reason why the national procedure

which has resulted in the establishment of a happy social state by the fusion in amity of once hostile tribes should not be extended to the creation of a wide comity of nations . . .

Misunderstandings and petty quarrels between individuals often occur in even the happiest family; but they are composed amicably, without resort to knife or pistol. So should it be in the case of bickering between nations.[13]

At another time, he said, 'The fruits of victory are perishable; and, at their best, are unsatisfying . . . as civilization goes on, war will be less and less popular; its pomp and glory are already tarnished and fading.'[14]

In his rectorial address at Edinburgh University three years before the outbreak of the Second World War, Allenby said that 'world organization, world consultation and co-operation are essential to world prosperity and international peace; as essential for the nations of the world to-day as for the thirteen independent, competitive and self-centred states of America in the 18th century'.[15]

On 7 August 1919 Allenby forwarded a recommendation that 'Abdu'l-Bahá be awarded a knighthood (KBE) for help and advice given to the civil administration of Palestine. The Bahá'í leader accepted the offer as 'a gift from a just king' but never used the title.[16]

General Allenby was honoured with a hereditary peerage, choosing the title 'Viscount Allenby of Megiddo and Felixtowe'.

18

The Road to Peace

. . . these fruitless strifes, these ruinous wars shall pass away, and the 'Most Great Peace' shall come . . .

Bahá'u'lláh[1]

When the slaughter of the war had reached its height, 'Abdu'l-Bahá had been filled with anguish. He prayed:

> O God, my God! Thou seest how black darkness is enshrouding all regions, how all countries are burning with the flame of dissension, and the fire of war and carnage is blazing throughout the East and the West. Blood is flowing, corpses bestrew the ground, and severed heads are fallen on the dust of the battlefield.[2]

He had looked forward, even at that time, firm in the belief that 'the Most Great Peace' which Bahá'u'lláh had promised would come:

> . . . the wisdom of this war is this: That it may become proven to all that the fire of war is world-consuming, whereas the rays of peace are world-enlightening. One is death, the other is life . . . one is the destroyer of the foundation of man, the other is the founder of the prosperity of the human race.[3]

In Paris, delegations were gathering with the stated aim of establishing peace through an international treaty. Some thought that the proposed 'League of Nations' might lead to the establishment of the Universal Peace of which 'Abdu'l-Bahá had spoken.[4] But the peace conference was becoming bogged down in controversy and self interest.

The Bahá'í leader wrote of the conference:

> Although the representatives of various governments are assembled in Paris in order to lay the foundations of Universal Peace and thus bestow rest and comfort upon the world of humanity, yet misunderstanding among some individuals is still predominant and self-interest still prevails. In such an atmosphere, Universal Peace will not be practicable, nay rather, fresh difficulties will arise. This is because interests are conflicting and aims are at variance . . .[5]

In December 1919 'Abdu'l-Bahá received a message from the Executive Committee of the Central Organization for a Durable Peace which had been written more than three years before. His response, a letter of far-reaching importance, was dispatched to its headquarters in the Hague by the hand of a special delegation.[6]

Once again 'Abdu'l-Bahá outlined the principles of Bahá'u'lláh, the essential prerequisites for a lasting peace. He also commented on the measures that had already been taken:

> . . . although the League of Nations has been brought into existence, yet it is incapable of establishing universal peace. But the Supreme Tribunal which His Holiness Bahá'u'lláh has described will fulfil this sacred task with the utmost might and power.[7]

When Italy invaded Abyssinia in 1935, the League of
Nations was powerless to take action. At that point its
authority collapsed. After the Second World War the
United Nations was born – a second attempt at securing a
permanent peace.

'Abdu'l-Bahá passed away in 1921. His funeral was
attended by at least ten thousand people from all the religious and ethnic communities in the Holy Land. Following
the coffin were the High Commissioner of Palestine, the
Governor of Jerusalem, the Governor of Phoenicia, the
chief officials of the government, consuls of several countries, the heads of the various religious communities, the
notables of Palestine, Jews, Christians, Muslims, Druses,
Egyptians, Turks, Kurds, Americans and Europeans.[8]

A well known Muslim was first to speak. 'Weep one
hour', he said, 'for the sake of him who, for well nigh
eighty years, hath wept for you! . . . Woe unto the poor, for
lo! goodness hath departed from them, woe unto the
orphans, for their loving father is no more with them!'[9]

The next speaker was a Christian. 'I weep for the
world,' he lamented, 'in that my Lord hath died . . . It is
not only our country's loss but a world affliction . . .'[10]

For the Jewish community, one of the leading figures in
Haifa spoke:

It is indeed strange that in an age of gross materialism
and lack of faith a great philosopher such as He whom we
mourn – 'Abdu'l-Bahá 'Abbás – should appear. He speaks
to our hearts, our consciences. He satisfies our thirsty
souls with teachings and principles that are the basis of all
religion and morality . . . His life was the living example
of self-sacrifice, of preferring the good of others to one's

own . . . He, Who has left such a glorious heritage, is not dead. He, Who has promulgated such great principles, is immortal in the memory of posterity.[11]

'Abdu'l-Bahá's call for universal peace did not die when the nations descended into the First World War, nor when the League of Nations failed, nor with the outbreak of the Second World War, nor with the shortcomings of the United Nations.

The principles of peace which 'Abdu'l-Bahá outlined are every bit as relevant today. Indeed some of them, which were highly contentious in His own time, have now become generally accepted.

The Bahá'í community, now numbering millions of adherents throughout the world, continues to follow the example of 'Abdu'l-Bahá, promoting unity and peace and reiterating the same principles – the equality of the sexes, the eradication of extreme poverty, the abolition of prejudices, the provision of education for all, the use of consultation as a means of decision-making and the establishment of a democratic world government, powerful enough to enforce a comprehensive code of international law.

'I came from a distant land,' 'Abdu'l-Bahá said.

I have travelled twenty thousand miles until I came to you . . . After all these long years of the sufferings of prison life I willingly took upon myself all the hardships of a long journey. Now I am here in order to be united with you, in order to meet you. My purpose is that perchance you may illumine the world of humanity; that all men may unite in perfect love and friendship; that religious prejudices, national prejudices, race distinctions, all may be completely abandoned . . . Think of the turmoil that today exists in the Balkans; how much blood is shed; how many thousands of mothers have lost their sons, how many children have become orphans, and how many buildings, villages, and cities have been destroyed! The Balkan states have become a volcano. All this ruin originates from the prejudices created by the different dogmas, called forth by superstitions and race prejudices.

... Strive and work so that the standard of the world of human Oneness may be raised among men, so that the lights of universal peace may shine and the East and the West embrace, and the material world become a mirror of the Kingdom of God, that eternal light may shine forth and that the day [may] break which will not be followed by night ... [12]

Bibliography

'Abdu'l-Bahá. *The Promulgation of Universal Peace*. Wilmette, Ill.: Bahá'í Publishing Trust, 1982.

—— *Tablets of the Divine Plan*. Wilmette, Ill.: Bahá'í Publishing Trust, 1977.

'Abdu'l-Bahá in London. London: Bahá'í Publishing Trust, 1987.

Aaronsohn, Alexander. *With the Turks in Palestine*. London: Constable and Co., 1917.

The Allenby Papers. Held by the Liddell Hart Centre for Military Archives, Kings College, London.

Allenby's Rectorial Address at Edinburgh 1936. A copy is held by the Liddell Hart Centre for Miliary Archives, Kings College, London.

Balyuzi, H. M. *'Abdu'l-Bahá*. Oxford: George Ronald, 1971.

Blomfield, Lady [Sara Louise]. *The Chosen Highway*. Wilmette, Ill.: Bahá'í Publishing Trust, 1967.

Bullock, David L. *Allenby's War: The Palestine-Arabian Campaigns 1916-18*. London: Blandford Press, 1988.

Compilation of Compilations, The. Prepared by the Universal House of Justice 1963-1990. 2 vols. [Sydney]: Bahá'í Publications Australia, 1991.

Djemal Pasha. *Memoirs of a Turkish Statesman, 1913-1919*. London: Hutchinson and Co., 1922.

Edmonds, Sir James E. *A Short History of World War I*. Oxford: Oxford University Press, 1951.

Esslemont, J. E. *Bahá'u'lláh and the New Era*. London: Bahá'í Publishing Trust, 1974.

Falls, Cyril (Benthan). *Armageddon 1918*. London: Weidenfeld and Nicolson, 1964.

Forman, Henry James. *The Story of Prophecy*. London: Cassell, 1936.

Gardner, Brian. *Allenby*. London: Cassell, 1965.

Gribbon, Walter. *Agents of Empire*. London: Blassey's (UK), 1995.

Idriess, I.L. *The Desert Column*. Sydney: Augus and Robertson Ltd., 1932.

Ives, Howard Colby. *Portals to Freedom*. London: George Ronald, 1967.

James, Lawrence. *Imperial Warrior*. London: Weidenfeld and Nicolson, 1993.

Lawrence, Thomas Edward. *The Seven Pillars of Wisdom*. London: Jonathan Cape, 1949.

MacMunn, George, and Cyril (Benthan) Falls. *The First World War. Military Operations: Egypt and Palestine*. vols. 1 and 2. London: H.M. Stationary Office, 1928–30.

Maḥmúd-i-Zarqání. *Maḥmúd's Diary*. Oxford: George Ronald, 1998.

Massey, W.T. *Allenby's Final Triumph*. London: Constable and Co., 1920.

Meinertzhagen, Richard. *Army Diary 1899–1926*. Edinburgh: Oliver and Boyd, 1960.

—— *Middle East Diary 1917 to 1956*.

Memories of David John Hughes. Private communication.

Momen, Moojan. *The Bábí and Bahá'í Religions, 1844–1944. Some Contemporary Western Accounts*. Oxford: George Ronald, 1981.

Momen, Wendi. *A Basic Bahá'í Dictionary*. Oxford: George Ronald, 1989.

Nabíl-i-A'zam. *The Dawn-Breakers: Nabíl's Narrative of the Early Days of the Bahá'í Revelation*. Wilmette, Ill.: Bahá'í Publishing Trust, 1970.

New Jerusalem Bible.

New World Translation of the Christian Scriptures.

Osborn, Rex. 'Operations of the Mounted Troops of the Egyptian Expeditionary Force'. *The Cavalry Journal*. London: Royal United Services Institute, vols. 1922 and 1923.

Sachar, Howard M. *Emergence of the Middle East 1914–1924*. New York: Alfred A. Knopf, 1969.

von Sanders, Liman. 'Turkish Operations in Palestine, 19th–23rd September, 1918'. *Royal United Services Institute Journal*. vol. 66, 1921.

Savage, Raymond. *Allenby of Armageddon*. Indianapolis: Bobbs-Merrill Co., 1926.

Shoghi Effendi. *The World Order of Bahá'u'lláh*. Wilmette, Ill.: Bahá'í Publishing Trust, 1991.

Star of the West. Rpt. Oxford: George Ronald, 1984.

Storrs, Sir Ronald. *Orientations*. London: Nicholson and Watson, 1943.

Thompson, Juliet. *'Abdu'l-Bahá the Center of the Covenant*. Wilmette, Ill.: Bahá'í Publishing Committee, 1948.

Tudor Pole, Wellesley. *The Silent Road*. London: Neville Spearman, 1960.

—— *Writing on the Ground*. London: Neville Spearman, 1968.

Ward, Allan L. *239 Days*. Wilmette, Ill.: Bahá'í Publishing Trust, 1979.

Wavell, Viscount, George G. *Allenby, Soldier and Statesman*. London: Harper and Co, 1946.

Weber, Frank George. *Eagles on the Crescent*. Ithaca: Cornell University Press, 1970.

Weinberg, Robert. *Ethel Jenner Rosenberg*. Oxford: George Ronald, 1995.

Wilson, Robert Henry. *Palestine 1917*. ed. Helen Millgate. Tunbridge Wells: Costello, 1987.

Yazdi, Ali. M. *Blessings Beyond Measure: Recollections of 'Abdu'l-Bahá and Shoghi Effendi*. Wilmette, Ill.: Bahá'í Publishing Trust, 1988.

Notes and References

Chapter 1: The Soldier's Vision

1. The biblical quotations are all taken from the *New Jerusalem Bible*.
2. MacMunn and Falls, *First World War. Military Operations: Egypt and Palestine*, vol. 1, pp. 229–36.
3. Gardner, *Allenby*, pp. 162-3.
4. Tudor Pole, *Silent Road*, p. 135.
5. ibid. p. 136.
6. ibid. pp. 136–7.
7. MacMunn and Falls, *First World War. Military Operations: Egypt and Palestine*, vol. 1, pp. 229-36.
8. Tudor Pole, *Silent Road*, p. 137.
9. ibid. pp. 134–8.
10. Shoghi Effendi, *God Passes By*, p. 306.

Chapter 2: The Servant

1. Balyuzi, *'Abdu'l-Bahá*, p. 3.
2. Quoted in Shoghi Effendi, *World Order*, p. 139.
3. Balyuzi, *'Abdu'l-Bahá*, p. 123.
4. ibid. p. 381.
5. Quoted in Balyuzi, *'Abdu'l-Bahá*, p. 138.
6. *The Times* of London, 6 September 1911.
7. *'Abdu'l-Bahá in London*, p. 19.
8. *The Times* of London, 27 September 1911.
9. ibid. 12 September 1911.
10. *'Abdu'l-Bahá in London*, pp. 19–20.
11. ibid. p. 106.
12. Quoted in Balyuzi, *'Abdu'l-Bahá*, p. 162.
13. For a chronicle of 'Abdu'l-Bahá's travels in America see Maḥmúd-i-Zarqání, *Maḥmúd's Diary*.

14. Quoted in Ward, *239 Days*, pp. 101–2.
15. ibid. pp. 15–16.
16. *Star of the West*, vol. 3, no. 7, pp. 5, 11.
17. Quoted in Ward, *239 Days*, p. 15.
18. 'Abdu'l-Bahá, *Promulgation*, p. 108.
19. Quoted in Balyuzi, *'Abdu'l-Bahá*, p. 347.
20. 'Abdu'l-Bahá, *Promulgation*, p. 122.
21. ibid. p. 322.
22. Ward, *239 Days*, pp. 170–1.
23. 'Abdu'l-Bahá, *Promulgation*, p. 376.
24. 'Abdu'l-Bahá, cited in Esslemont, *Bahá'u'lláh and the New Era*, p. 223.
25. Balyuzi, *'Abdu'l-Bahá*, p. 406.
26. Shoghi Effendi, *God Passes By*, p. 281.

Chapter 3: The General

 1. Bullock, *Allenby's War*, p. 9.
 2. 'Abdu'l-Bahá, *Tablets of the Divine Plan*, p. 22.
 3. ibid. pp. 22–3.
 4. Quoted in Gardner, *Allenby*, p. 40.
 5. ibid. pp. 31–2.
 6. ibid. p. 23.
 7. ibid. p. 35.
 8. ibid. p. 40.
 9. ibid. pp. 59–60.
10. Quoted in James, *Imperial Warrior*, p. 94.
11. Quoted in Wavell, *Allenby, Soldier and Statesman*, p. 144.
12. James, *Imperial Warrior*, p. 95.
13. Gardner, *Allenby*, p. 103.
14. Quoted in Savage, *Allenby of Armageddon*, p. 171.
15. Quoted in James, *Imperial Warrior*, p. 100.
16. Edmonds, *A Short History of World War I*, p. 234.

Chapter 4: Sinai

 1. Quoted in Sachar, *Emergence of the Middle East*, p. 21.
 2. Djemal Pasha, *Memoirs of a Turkish Statesman*, pp. 150-1.

3. Quoted in Idriess, *Desert Column*, p. 145.
4. ibid. p. 71.
5. ibid. pp. 68–9, 83.
6. ibid. p. 96.
7. Exodus 17:3.
8. Quoted in Idriess, *Desert Column*, p. 177.
9. Djemal Pasha, *Memoirs of a Turkish Statesman*, p. 179.
10. Idriess, *Desert Column*, pp. 187–97.

Chapter 5: The Promised Land

1. Quoted in Gardner, *Allenby*, p. 111.
2. Quoted in James, *Imperial Warrior*, p. 93.
3. Quoted in Gardner, *Allenby*, p. 114.
4. Before his death in 1843, Siyyid Kázim-i-Rashtí, a renowned Islamic teacher of the Shaykhí school, indicated that the time for the appearance of the Promised One was at hand. But he warned that only through prayerful endeavour, purity of motive and singleness of mind could He be found. As a result, several of Siyyid Kázim's followers set out in search. For a detailed description of this episode see Nabíl-i-A'zam, *Dawn-Breakers*, chs. 2–3.

Chapter 6: Famine and Plague

1. One shell overshot its target, a bridge over a river, and landed on an island further upstream. A garden had, some years earlier, been prepared on the island by 'Abdu'l-Bahá for the use of Bahá'u'lláh. The garden was named 'Ridván'. The shell failed to explode. See Balyuzi, *'Abdu'l-Bahá*, p. 411.
2. Aaronsohn, *With the Turks in Palestine*, p. 93.
3. Thompson, *'Abdu'l-Bahá*, p. 10.
4. 'Abdu'l-Bahá, *Promulgation*, p. 217.
5. Blomfield, *Chosen Highway*, pp. 209–10.
6. Gribbon, *Agents of Empire*, p. 116.
7. Letter of Mirza Ahmad Sohrab, in *Star of the West*, vol. 9, no. 17, p. 191.
8. Gribbon, *Agents of Empire*, pp. 116–17.

9. ibid. p. 126.
10. Aaronsohn, *With the Turks in Palestine*, p. 71.
11. Djemal Pasha, *Memoirs of a Turkish Statesman*, p. 202.
12. Gribbon, *Agents of Empire*, p. 110.
13. Aaronsohn, *With the Turks in Palestine*, p. 42.
14. Blomfield, *Chosen Highway*, pp. 209–10.
15. Djemal Pasha, *Memoirs of a Turkish Statesman*, p. 151.
16. Aaronsohn, *With the Turks in Palestine*, p. 63.
17. Ives, *Portals to Freedom*, pp. 128–9.
18. Aaronsohn, *With the Turks in Palestine*, chapter 7.

Chapter 7: Deception
1. Meinertzhagen, *Army Diary 1899–1926*, p. 216.
2. Momen, *Basic Bahá'í Dictionary*, p. 219.
3. Blomfield, *Chosen Highway*, pp. 206–8.
4. ibid. p. 210.
5. Yazdi, *Blessings Beyond Measure*, p. 25.
6. 'Abdu'l-Bahá, in *Compilation*, vol. 2, pp. 339–40, no. 2058.
7. 'Abdu'l-Bahá, *Promulgation*, p. 288.
8. See Meinertzhagen, *Army Diary 1899–1926*, pp. 216–19.

Chapter 8: The Battle for Gaza
1. Savage, *Allenby of Armageddon*, p. 273.
2. Quoted in Wavell, *Allenby, Soldier and Statesman*, p. 79.
3. Savage, *Allenby of Armageddon*, p. 194.
4. Quoted in Idriess, *Desert Column*, p. 237.
5. Meinertzhagen, *Middle East Diary 1917 to 1956*, pp. 28–9.
6. Lawrence, *Seven Pillars of Wisdom*, p. 330.
7. Djemal Pasha, *Memories of a Turkish Statesman*, p. 180.
8. ibid. p. 172.
9. Savage, *Allenby of Armageddon*, p. 215.
10. Meinertzhagen, *Army Diary 1899–1926*, pp. 284–5.
11. Quoted in Wilson, *Palestine 1917*, p. 92.
12. Aaronsohn, *With the Turks in Palestine*, pp. 65–6.

Chapter 9: The Waters of the Nile

1. Forman, *Story of Prophecy*, p. 95.
2. Wavell, *Allenby, Soldier and Statesman*, p. 170.
3. Exodus 17:6.
4. 'Memories of David John Hughes', private communication, p. 137.
5. ibid.
6. Savage, *Allenby of Armageddon*, p. 276.
7. Quoted in Wilson, *Palestine 1917*, p. 95.
8. 'Memories of David John Hughes', private communication, pp. 139–41.
9. Blomfield, *Chosen Highway*, p. 228.
10. Savage, *Allenby of Armageddon*, p. 258.

Chapter 10: Djemal Pasha

1. Biyuk Djemal Pasha (Djemal Pasha the greater) should not be confused with Muhammad Djemal Pasha (Djemal Pasha the lesser), a very competent general who was in command of the Turkish 4th Army after the fall of Jerusalem.
2. Sachar, *Emergence of the Middle East 1914–1924*, p. 121.
3. Pasha is not a name but a military title.
4. Djemal Pasha, *Memoirs of a Turkish Statesman*, p. 219.
5. Yazdi, *Blessings Beyond Measure*, p. 32.
6. Gribbon, *Agents of Empire*, p. 116.
7. Balyuzi, *'Abdu'l-Bahá*, p. 413.
8. Sachar, *Emergence of the Middle East 1914–1924*, p. 159.
9. Weber, *Eagles on the Crescent*, p. 136.
10. Balyuzi, *'Abdu'l-Bahá*, pp. 413–14.
11. Shoghi Effendi, *God Passes By*, p. 306. There is some doubt about the circumstances which would have triggered the death sentence. Blomfield's *The Chosen Highway* states on page 220 that a date was set for the execution. Balyuzi in *'Abdu'l-Bahá* states on page 414 that it was to be carried out when the Pasha returned victorious from his campaign. Whatever the specific details, it is clear that 'Abdu'l-Bahá's life was in real danger – a danger which would have become even greater in the chaotic

conditions accompanying a British advance towards Haifa
and during any changeover of administration.

Chapter 11: The Valley of Death
1. Wilson, *Palestine 1917*, pp. 108–110.
2. ibid. p. 108.
3. ibid. p. 109.
4. Falls, *Armageddon 1918*, p. 172.
5. Wavell, *Allenby, Soldier and Statesman*, p. 216.
6. Wilson, *Palestine 1917*, pp. 105–6.
7. 'Memories of David John Hughes', private communication.
   pp. 153–4.

Chapter 12: The War Cabinet
1. Quoted in Momen, *Bábí and Bahá'í Religions 1844–1944*, p. 333.
2. ibid. p. 332.
3. Blomfield, *Chosen Highway*, p. 222.
4. Gardner, *Allenby*, p. 176.
5. Weinberg, *Ethel Jenner Rosenberg*, p. 169.
6. Quoted in Momen, *Bábí and Bahá'í Religions 1844–1944*,
   p. 333.
7. Quoted in ibid. p. 334.
8. ibid.
9. Quoted in Blomfield, *Chosen Highway*, p. 223.
10. ibid.

Chapter 13: Inspiration
1. The Allenby Papers, no. 1/12/26.
2. The Allenby Papers, no. 1/12/32.
3. 'Abdu'l-Bahá, *Tablets of the Divine Plan*, pp. 22–3:
   During my stay in America I cried out in every meeting
   and summoned the people to the propagation of the
   ideals of universal peace. I said plainly that the continent
   of Europe had become like unto an arsenal and its confla-
   gration was dependent upon one spark, and that in the
   coming years, or within two years, all that which is

recorded in the Revelation of John and the Book of
Daniel would become fulfilled and come to pass.
4. 'Abdu'l-Bahá, *Promulgation*, p. 102.
5. Massey, *Allenby's Final Triumph*, pp. 98–102.
6. Lawrence, *Seven Pillars of Wisdom*, p. 604.
7. *The Cavalry Journal 1922*, p. 354.
8. Falls, *First World War. Military Operations: Egypt and Palestine*,
   vol. 2, p. 468.

Chapter 14: Armageddon
1. Wilson, *Palestine 1917*, p. 123.
2. Massey, *Allenby's Final Triumph*, p. 119.
3. *The Cavalry Journal 1923*, p. 21.
4. Falls, *The First World War. Military Operations: Egypt and Palestine*,
   vol. 2, p. 468.
5. There are several descriptions of this vital skirmish, not all of
   which agree. Savage's *Allenby of Armageddon* states on page 207
   that the leading unit 'discovered a Turkish force with several
   machine-guns racing to hold the pass', which suggests that the
   Turks had no time to prepare for the attack. Falls's *Armageddon
   1918* gives on page 93 a full description of the fighting, which
   suggests that the Turks were dug in around the mouth of the
   pass.
6. Savage, *Allenby of Armageddon*, p. 300.
7. Wilson, *Palestine 1917*, p. 130.
8. von Sanders, 'Turkish Operations in Palestine', *Royal United
   Services Institute Journal*, vol. 66, 1921, p. 334.
9. Wilson, *Palestine 1917*, p. 135.

Chapter 15: The Most Terrible Plague
1. A talent was approximately 113 lbs. *New World Translation of the
   Christian Scriptures*.
2. It is interesting to note that these bombs dropped at the climax
   of the battle of Armageddon weighed 112 lbs, while the 'great
   hailstones' mentioned at the climax of chapter 16 of the Book
   of Revelation weighed approximately 113 lbs.

3. Bullock, *Allenby's War*, p. 135.
4. Massey, *Allenby's Final Triumph*, p. 185.
5. Isaiah 34:2–3.

Chapter 16: The Battle for Haifa

1. 'Abdu'l-Bahá, *Tablets of the Divine Plan*, p. 57.
2. Massey, *Allenby's Final Triumph*, p. 189.
3. Tudor Pole, *Writing on the Ground*, p. 154.
4. ibid. pp. 157–8.
5. ibid. p. 158.
6. Wilson, *Palestine 1917*, pp. 136–7.
7. Balyuzi, *'Abdu'l-Bahá*, p. 430.
8. Quoted in Momen, *Bábí and Bahá'í Religions 1844–1944*, p. 337.
9. Blomfield, *Chosen Highway*, p. 210.
10. Quoted in Balyuzi, *'Abdu'l-Bahá*, pp. 431–2.

Chapter 17: The Eleventh Hour

1. Wilson, *Palestine 1917*, p. 141.
2. ibid.
3. Sachar, *Emergence of the Middle East 1914–1924*, p. 242.
4. Lawrence, *Seven Pillars of Wisdom*, p. 674.
5. Wilson, *Palestine 1917*.
6. Massey, *Allenby's Final Triumph*, p. 309.
7. Gardner, *Allenby*, p. 194.
8. Sachar, *Emergence of the Middle East 1914–1924*, p. 249.
9. Meinertzhagen, *Middle East Diary 1817–1956*, p. 45.
10. Weinberg, *Ethel Jenner Rosenberg*, pp. 213–14, p. 286.
11. Storrs, *Orientations*, p. 320.
12. Quoted in Tudor Pole, *Writing on the Ground*, pp. 158–9.
13. Allenby's Rectorial Address at Edinburgh 1936, p. 10.
14. The Allenby Papers, no. 3/5.
15. Allenby's Rectorial Address at Edinburgh 1936, p. 10.
16. Balyuzi, *'Abdu'l-Bahá*, p. 443.

Chapter 18: The Road to Peace

1. Bahá'u'lláh, in *Compilation*, vol. 2, p. 157, no. 1578.

2. 'Abdu'l-Bahá, *Tablets of the Divine Plan*, pp. 56–7.
3. ibid. p. 55.
4. See, for example, Weinberg, *Ethel Jenner Rosenberg*, p. 167.
5. 'Abdu'l-Bahá, quoted in Balyuzi, *'Abdu'l-Bahá*, pp. 437–8.
6. Shoghi Effendi, *God Passes By*, p. 308.
7. 'Abdu'l-Bahá, *Selections*, p. 306.
8. Balyuzi, *'Abdu'l-Bahá*, pp. 464–5.
9. Quoted in ibid. pp. 466–7.
10. Quoted in ibid. p. 467.
11. Quoted in ibid. pp. 471–2.
12. Quoted in ibid. pp. 381–2.

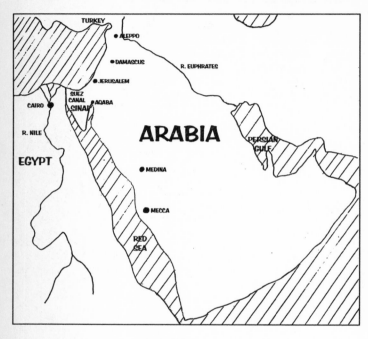

Map 1
Arabia and the Levant

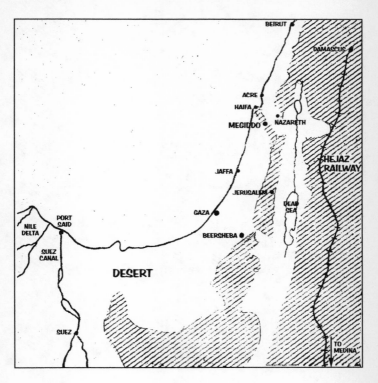

Map 2
The Route of the Hejaz Railway

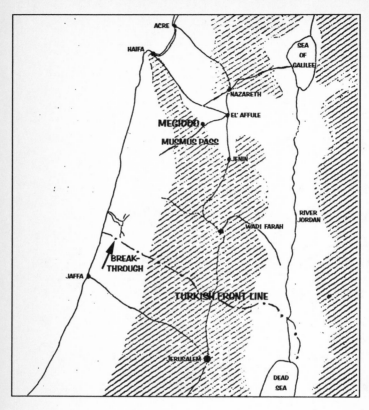

Map 3
The Turkish Front Line